THE SAVAGE LEADER

13 PRINCIPLES TO BECOME A BETTER LEADER FROM THE INSIDE OUT

DARREN REINKE

ISBN 978-1-7361179-0-3

Published by Group Sixty Publishing

Cover Design by Randy Hernandez
Cover Photo Credit: Prince David on Unsplash.com

To my beautiful wife, Melissa and our boys, Madden and Kai for believing in me and for being the guiding light and inspiration in my life.

The Savage Leader Field Guide

To drive the adoption of the 13 Savage Principles, I created *The Savage Leader Field Guide* that you can use as you go through the book. Download your complimentary guide at: TheSavageLeader.com

CONTENTS

INTRODUCTION 1

SAVAGE PRINCIPLE #1 17

SAVAGE PRINCIPLE #2 30

SAVAGE PRINCIPLE #3 36

SAVAGE PRINCIPLE #4 47

SAVAGE PRINCIPLE #5 58

SAVAGE PRINCIPLE #6 66

SAVAGE PRINCIPLE #7 75

SAVAGE PRINCIPLE #8 86

SAVAGE PRINCIPLE #9 97

SAVAGE PRINCIPLE #10 107

SAVAGE PRINCIPLE #11 115

SAVAGE PRINCIPLE #12 123

SAVAGE PRINCIPLE #13 133

CONCLUSION 142

SOURCES 144

ACKNOWLEDGEMENTS 149

AUTHOR BIO 151

INTRODUCTION

"Be a leader."

Most of us hear this phrase. It's a message no longer reserved just for the aspiring C-suite executive or CEO. It's for everyone from the recent college graduate to the mid-career professional to the top of the corporate ladder. It's for every industry and every sector too.

But what does it mean to be a leader? How do we become one? What does it take?

Business schools, corporate training programs, and continuing education classes largely focus on teaching us leadership traits that are externally visible. We learn decision making and how to evaluate risk. We learn how to develop a business strategy and to set a vision. We learn how to motivate employees and teams, and how to improve productivity, create efficiencies, and find cost reductions.

These are vital skills. As a proud and active alumni board member at the Haas School of Business at UC Berkley, where I earned my MBA, I am grateful for what I learned there, and in the halls at large companies including Accenture, Gap, and Neutrogena. For the last decade, I've worked as an executive coach and consultant to aspiring and current CEOs, entrepreneurs, C-suite executives, and leadership teams. I know how important the hard skills are, but they are only the tip of the iceberg—the real work to becoming a leader lies beneath the surface.

We don't create leaders from the outside in; we build leaders from the inside out.

To become a leader, we have to look within ourselves to see what internal anchors—self-limiting beliefs, doubts, or fears—are holding us back from achieving our goals. We have to know our values and then learn how to align our decisions with them. We have to become comfortable and confident in who we are—as people and as leaders—so we bring our authentic and genuine selves into our careers. We have to become bold in our choices, in taking risks that can lead us to experiencing greater fulfillment and purpose in our work.

This is the inner game that many of us have to learn through trial and error because there are no programs teaching us how to acknowledge, let alone navigate our inner journeys.

This is knowledge we need to succeed professionally (and in life). Without understanding what's going on internally, we can easily become rudderless. We may second-guess career and business decisions. We may make poor choices that don't align with our values. We may allow external pressures and people to shape who we are and how we engage with our colleagues and teams. We may get frustrated when projects or opportunities take longer than we had expected, or we may become devastated with disappointments that inevitably hit our shores.

This was David's story. When I met David, he believed he needed to become the leader that his CEO thought he should become. David was a senior executive at a major global life sciences firm. His responsibilities had him rubbing elbows with some of the highest-ranking politicians and senior government officials in the United States. During one performance review, David's CEO—who he reported to—gave David feedback saying that he needed to work on his "executive presence." According to the CEO, David was too humble.

Aspiring to be the next CEO, David took the feedback to heart. He vowed to work on his executive presence and to stop being humble, if that was what it would take for him to reach the top.

Except, it wasn't going to work. His two biggest values were humility and authenticity, so to strip those away would be to take away who David is at his core. He is one of the most genuine and authentic people you'll ever meet. He comes across as sincere and mild-mannered, yet strong because he fundamentally believes in his organization and its purpose. David is mission-driven, and his passion comes through. He's empathetic, a fantastic listener, and he puts people at ease. He isn't braggadocios—but he doesn't have to be.

David's challenge wasn't to mold himself in the image of his CEO and to develop his CEO's style of executive presence, it was to tap into David's core and unleash his inner leader.

When David came to work with me, we focused on helping him develop his own style and to stand proudly in his authenticity. When David learned to do that, he started to reach a level of success previously not achievable for him. He completed challenging and long-stalled projects that his firm had previously not been able to push over the finish line. He broadened his network and developed key relationships with community stakeholders critical to his firm's success.

The more confident David felt, the more assertive he became. The more assertive he was, the more confident he felt. This self-fulfilling loop gave David a certain light. He held himself differently. He felt more sure of who he was, his role, and the contribution and value he brought to the company. As this transformation happened, something interesting developed: David's CEO noticed. Instead of badgering David to become flashier, the CEO admitted that different leadership styles could be effective, and that maybe, David (and others) could be their authentic selves and still achieve the firm's mission. Today, David continues to embrace his authentic leadership style and remains in the running to become the successor to the current CEO.

THE BIRTH OF THE SAVAGE LEADER

I have always been fascinated in leadership, what it meant, and how to become a leader. I can still hear my mom's voice saying, "Darren, be a leader!"

At the time, I didn't understand what she meant, but now I realize it was her way of reminding me to resist peer pressure and to act on my principles. It was also how she challenged me to be my best. She wasn't preparing me for the day when I would take a leadership role in business. She was preparing me to be the best leader and person that I could be—one who would lead by example, inspire others to change and grow, and to make a difference in all areas of my life. My mom wanted me to be a person who could and would make the right choices and do what was right, even if that meant taking a personal risk and standing apart from my peers.

I stepped onto the business path while earning my undergrad degree at UC Davis. Early in my career, I thought the business world would teach me the truth about leadership and how to become a leader. I had a front row seat at what leadership looked like in corporate America. First, I worked in the process group at Accenture before earning my MBA and sliding into the strategy consulting world. I've worked at Fortune 500 companies Gap and Neutrogena (Owned by Johnson & Johnson), and I've managed major corporate clients including Dell EMC, Dow, E*Trade, Kaiser Permanente, and Adecco.

Unfortunately, my time in corporate America left me largely disillusioned with the work and some of the "leaders." The bloated bureaucracy frustrated me, and it was disheartening to see great ideas—from me and my colleagues—get watered down through layers of executive feedback. The forced employee performance reviews on a human bell curve made no sense to me, and I was frustrated by the lack of control over my schedule and life.

I encountered leaders who were often promoted despite being largely inauthentic, untrustworthy, too busy for mentoring, and egotistical to a degree that didn't allow for collaboration or cooperation. I've also met quite a few hypocrites, who have built reputations saying all the right stuff, but who were terrors behind the scenes.

There has to be a better way, I often thought. Thankfully, I met a few incredible leaders who showed me such leadership was possible. But these men and women were in the minority.

As I moved upward within organizations, I was often asked to lead even when I didn't have the official title. I tended to mentor naturally—it was a core strength—so when I left the corporate ranks to follow the entrepreneur trail, it felt natural to start my own executive coaching and training company, Group Sixty.

For over a decade, my firm has specialized in strengthening teams and organizations by transforming leaders and managers into player-coaches who can engage, develop, and promote their direct reports. In my client work, we coach leaders and their teams to improve communication, collaboration, trust, and accountability that leads to greater productivity and lower turnover from the top down. We also help leaders on their "inner journey" to unleash their potential by tackling self-limiting beliefs, doubts, and fears while becoming more values-centric and authentic.

Our work blends the traditional disciplines of management consulting, executive coaching, and personal branding so that we can seamlessly pivot from coaching conversations focused on soft skills to sessions around high-level business strategy and execution.

My work has taken me into diverse institutions and industries, and I've coached people in different positions—from early-stage start-ups to large, global companies to nonprofits and academia to the military. No matter where I go, everyone faces a similar challenge: how do they develop an authentic leadership style and become the best leader they can be?

Leadership styles vary. There is no one-size-fits-all path to become one. Yet, the question still remains: How do we become the leader we are meant to be—not some carbon-copy of someone else? I have doggedly pursued the answer to this question and others: What does it take to become a leader? What does it look like in today's world? What inner skills and traits must we harness to build our unique leadership style? And how can I help more people become better, more authentic leaders in their professional (and personal) lives?

These questions inspire much of my work today, and they led me to research and write this book. In my perpetual quest to understand leadership and how we create great leaders, I have spent the last decade examining what principles, traits, and characteristics set inspiring leaders apart from the mediocre ones.

I believe leadership transcends business, and we can learn a lot when we step outside our traditional arenas to watch and listen. That's why I've interviewed dozens of people in diverse sectors including leading executives, entrepreneurs, professional athletes, collegiate and professional athletic coaches, therapists, nonprofit executives, venture capitalists, military special forces including former Navy SEALs.

The more inspiring leaders I spoke to, the more patterns I saw emerge. Very few people highlighted the hard skills they had learned. Instead they talked about overcoming inner obstacles on their way to "greatness" as they defined it.

I soon began calling these men and women, *Savage Leaders*.

Savage Leaders are bold enough to face down their fears, overcome their doubts, and smash their self-limiting beliefs as they chase down their career (and life) goals. They don't shy away from change or challenges, instead they square their shoulders, stand tall, and walk toward the unknown with courage and fortitude. Savage Leaders are willing to go deep within themselves to uncover who they are, identify their unique strengths and talents, to admit their long-held aspirations, and then to go for them.

Savage Leaders learn to tap into their unique styles and abilities bringing authenticity to their every action and interaction with others. Savage Leaders care about their colleagues and teams and are determined to help them grow and develop. No matter what title sits next to someone's name, Savage Leaders believe everyone is a leader who deserves to be respected, listened to, and invested in. Savage Leaders make decisions based on their values and what is important to them.

Savage Leaders embrace the ongoing journey of growth and learning and relish developing new skills. And they know their purpose and mission in the world, working in service of it every day. Savage Leaders have an unquenchable thirst for "greatness," which is their way of saying they want to reach their potential and aspirations, whether that is to win an Iron Man race, leave their corporate job to start a company, run a successful bilingual school, or transition from a successful military career in an elite special-forces unit to a meaningful position in the civilian world.

I believe buried inside each of us is a Savage Leader—we just need to learn how to unlock and unleash them. When we do that, we become authentic leaders. We become more confident and assertive in our decision-making and how we engage with colleagues, managers, direct reports, and the teams we lead. We can better motivate and influence our teams. We become more productive and can realize a greater impact on our organizations. We can also experience more fulfillment, a sense of purpose, and greater enjoyment in our careers.

A NEW LEADERSHIP MODEL

Savage leaders differ from traditional leaders in many ways such as:

Traditional Leaders	Savage Leaders
Focuses on being successful	Aims for greatness, not just success
Is comfortable with the status quo	Constantly challenges the status quo and asks "why?" and "what if?" questions
Focuses on who they think they should be	Is confident in who they are, and is rooted in their values and beliefs
Focuses more on external rewards and achievements	Focuses first on the process, and then the outcomes
Leads with title, status, and credentials	Leads with strengths
Is resume focused	Is experience driven
Uses development to shore up weaknesses	Uses development to amplify strengths
Is rigid, and rules based	Is willing to challenge authority, rules, and norms
Fears failure	Embraces failure as part of the learning process
Believes hierarchy determines leadership	Believes leadership is everyone's responsibility

Traditional Leaders	Savage Leaders
Believes only managers/executives lead	Believes everyone possesses leadership ability
Plays it safe	Takes small risks rooted in growth
"Others solely determine my fate"	"I determine my fate, with the support of others"
Remains comfortable with a static set of skills and knowledge	Has an unquenchable thirst to learn new skills and acquire knowledge
Is surrounded by executives and leaders who "play it safe"	Creates a tribe of fellow Savage Leaders
"Copies and pastes" best practices	Tailors best practices into authentic "Savage Practices"
Is driven by ego	Is driven by purpose
Uses a command-and-control style with their team	Empowers and enables their team
Is steadfast and inflexible	Is nimble and agile
Seeks comfort in the past	Is comfortable amid change and uncertainty

BECOMING A SAVAGE LEADER

In the coming pages, I will introduce you to the *13 Savage Principles* that Savage Leaders embrace. When used together, these principles will give you a map and the tools and strategies you need to unleash the Savage Leader inside of you.

In every chapter, I've identified a common problem that we face in our professional lives. Then I dig into several traits that a Savage Leader may use to help overcome the situation. At the end of the chapter, you will find a challenge that you can use to bring the Savage Principle into your life now. You don't have to try every trait in each chapter; pick one that seems interesting and start there.

You can read this book from front cover to back or skip around. Some principles may resonate more strongly with you than others. Some principles may have direct application today while others may have more relevance a few months or even a year from now. Becoming a Savage Leader is a lifelong journey— enjoy it.

I've filled every chapter with stories from my career, and those of the amazing entrepreneurs, business executives, professional athletes and their coaches, elite military special forces, and other Savage Leaders who I've worked with, coached, and interviewed for this book.

Their stories offer us an opportunity to rethink the traditional qualities of leadership, and to reimagine what leadership can look like in today's world and in our own lives.

Every principle in this book, I have tried in my life. These are the ones that I keep returning to whenever I feel stuck, uncertain, or experience doubt. As my clients will attest, I'm in the trenches with them. I'm on a parallel journey, dealing with my own self-limiting beliefs, doubts, and fears. I feel discomfort when I publish blogs, post videos, or launch new coaching programs. But I keep pushing myself to reach my potential to "be a leader" like my mom told me, and to achieve my definition of "greatness" because I know it's the right path.

THREE ATTRIBUTES OF SAVAGE LEADERS

"Every day you are either getting better or getting worse. You never stay the same."
Bo Schembechler

I've found that Savage Leaders share three core attributes. If you have these, then the odds are that you'll be more successful in adopting the 13 Savage Principles.

Attribute #1: You Possess a Burning Desire to Achieve Your Own Definition of Greatness

Every one possesses the potential for greatness. For most of us, it's overwhelming to consider what that means. Everyone has the ability to be great, though everyone has a different definition of what that means.

If you asked basketball player, Steph Curry of the Golden State Warriors what his definition of greatness was at the beginning of his career, he would likely have talked about being the best shooter who ever lived. Though that statement might now be considered fact, today he might say that greatness is "being the best scorer that ever lived" or, "being the greatest team in NBA history."

Pose the same question to a Silicon Valley entrepreneur, and his response would probably center on creating a revolutionary product that transforms society, or to build the world's greatest company with a valuation on the order of Apple, Google, or other unicorn firms.

Ask a parent, and they may say that greatness to them is raising a well-balanced, confident, community-minded kid who is equipped to go into the world and achieve their dreams.

We all have different definitions of greatness. What yours is, is less important than that you have one. To fulfill your inner potential as a Savage Leader there must be an internal flame, or at least a spark that can eventually combust into a fire to achieve your greatness.

Not just be successful, but to be great!

If you picked up this book, I suspect you have a desire to be great. You probably have a set of goals that sit in thinner, rarified air. That's good. Lean into them. If you're unclear on your goals, but you just have this sense deep within that you want to "be great" then feed off that.

A desire to play a bigger game is a critical ingredient to becoming a Savage Leader. For some of you, the time might not be right to take that big step forward, though my hope is that the stories and tools provided in this book will help ignite that spark to be great or to remove those impediments which have stalled your efforts in the past.

Savage Leaders wake up every day with an incessant desire for forward progress—progress toward greatness.

Attribute #2: You're Willing to Be Introspective and Change

The second foundational attribute of a Savage Leader is a willingness to take an honest look inside themselves searching for, identifying, assessing, and evaluating their values, beliefs, drives, and strengths. They also constantly look for barriers in their path to achieving their goals.

The ability to be introspective and weaponize the potential inside of us is a critical, yet often overlooked part of leadership development. Gaining visibility and understanding of what lies within, provides both the motivation and insight to make the changes necessary to be great.

Being willing to look inside and change will be key to successfully applying the Savage Principles in this book. Without it, you will pay lip service to change and undercut your ability to become the leader you desire to be.

Savage Leaders regularly take a hard and honest look inside themselves to tap into what makes them great as well as to identify what needs changing.

Attribute #3: You're Willing to Put in the Work

The third element that all Savage Leaders have in common is a willingness to put in the work to get better. Without it, all the desire to be great and introspection in the world won't push you forward. The work is the spark that activates all of that desire and insight into tangible action and progress.

Growth and personal development take time and effort. The path forward isn't always smooth or straightforward. It's full of twists and turns, bumps, and times of prolonged effort without an immediate payoff. To grow and evolve, fears and doubts will inevitably arise that need addressing. The willingness to put in ongoing effort is the only way to persevere and achieve your goals.

My own life and career have been far from linear, but continuing to put in the effort each and every day while keeping an eye toward improving drives my quest toward my definition of great.

Savage Leaders are willing to put in the hard work in their quest to be great.

LEADERSHIP TO CHANGE THE WORLD?

We live in a time of profound, rapid, and accelerating change and disruption.

Even before the Coronavirus pandemic, technology and global competition were stressing companies like never before. Organizations of all sizes were scrambling to create greater agility enabled by new leadership models. Recently, Deloitte Consulting surveyed more than 10,000 human resources and business leaders across 140 countries. They found "companies are pushing the boundaries of their traditional leadership hierarchies, empowering a new breed of leaders who can thrive in a rapidly changing network."

I've had a front row seat, working with companies of all sizes and their leaders who have been challenged to reboot their traditional leadership paradigms. These leaders have worked to create new models that equip their people to unleash the leadership in others. For many C-suite executives, this was the path to addressing our persistently uncertain future.

Leadership needs to be driven into all tentacles of organizations, if they are to survive and thrive. I believe that, but that's only part of the answer.

Many of us have watched and lived through a period of profound leadership failures. The people who were appointed to guide us have let us down. I'm talking leaders of corporations. Leaders of non-profits. Leaders of academic institutions. Leaders in government.

The news cycle relentlessly exposes unethical and illegal behaviors by people entrusted to lead us. Think corporate scandals at Wells Fargo, Theranos, and Uber. Think hiring and pay bias issues at Fortune 500 behemoths, and sexual abuse reports that have led to resignations by giant moguls of the entertainment and sports industries and religious institutions. There's corruption in college basketball that in one instance, resulted in the University of Louisville having its victories and national title revoked, and athletes who lost college eligibility. We've seen admissions scandals too.

Cheating, lying, and harassment seem to have replaced traditional leadership competencies around trust, transparency, and accountability. These scandals have created a leadership vacuum.

Left unchecked, these toxic leadership models can trickle into our organizations and institutions, creating negative examples that get followed by the future leaders of our companies, in government, and in society.

If our organizations and communities are going to survive the current upheaval and thrive, I believe we need a different kind of leader. One who is self-aware, fiercely authentic, and driven by purpose. We need leaders willing to challenge the status quo, accept risk taking as a norm, and who learn from setbacks, mistakes, and failures. We need people to be bold and assertive, yet willing to listen, collaborate, and want to achieve greatness—both individually and collectively as a team and organization.

Old models rooted in veiled command-and-control leadership while paying lip service to organization-wide accountability are no longer sufficient to succeed in today's uncertain world. We need more Savage Leaders in our organizations—businesses, politics, non-profits, and governments. And we need more people at all levels, from the top of the organization down to the bottom, to find and embrace their Savage Leader within.

If we had more Savage Leaders, would this fix the world? That would be quite the audacious claim for me to make. While I don't know for sure, I do know that we need change and that will only come when the people inside our institutions do the changing. I'm curious and it's a world that I'd be interested in living in.

JUMP IN

This book isn't for the box checkers, or those people who subscribe to the status quo and its comforts. I work with the change makers, the rainmakers, the not-so-every-day people who strive to do more, be more, and experience more. This is a book for the status-quo challenging entrepreneur, the community activist, and the high-potential manager. It's for trailblazing teachers and educators, mid-level managers, and startup founders who want to inspire the next generation of leaders.

It's for anyone, just starting their careers to winding them down, who has a burning desire to reach their potential and to do it their way.

To achieve our own definitions of "greatness" in meeting external goals requires all the hard work and introspection detailed in the coming pages. Ultimately, becoming a Savage Leader requires an inner journey to defeat our self-limiting beliefs, doubts, and fears. It's about gaining clarity around who we are, who we want to be, what we want to achieve in our careers and lives, and then taking bold, decisive action.

We all want to reach our potential. We want to inspire our colleagues and teams. We want to be heard, seen, and to know that we're making a difference and having a real impact on our organizations. This is possible. It is attainable.

Your journey to becoming a Savage Leader starts now.

Let's get to it.

SAVAGE PRINCIPLE #1

USE VALUES TO ANCHOR AND GUIDE YOU

"It's not hard to make decisions when you know what your values are."

Roy Disney

Values guide our lives and careers.

They inform key decisions and influence how we lead our teams. They are the foundation for who we are, what we do, how we lead, and where we go. Unfortunately, many leaders either don't know or lack a strong set of values. Without them, leaders can find themselves at the whims of circumstance, suffering whiplash from decisions that lack anchoring.

I once worked with a leader, Jason who constantly chased the highest-profile projects within his firm as well as job opportunities with the richest rewards. While there is nothing wrong with these choices, Jason disregarded the downsides of these decisions, and he struggled with feeling like he had led an unfulfilled life.

It was only after Jason gained clarity about what mattered most to him—being a great developer and coach to his team— that Jason was able to more consistently make decisions that aligned with his values. He stopped focusing just on landing the biggest, most high-profile projects and pivoted to how he could help develop and impact more people. By acknowledging his values and aligning them with his work, he enjoyed more fulfillment and drove greater progress and development in his organization. He still landed big clients—that was a big part of his job—but he saw that work as an avenue to do all the other development and coaching that ignited him.

The best leaders know their values and live them.

"Use Values to Anchor and Guide You" is the first Savage Principle because it forms the foundation that enables you to successfully apply the other principles in this book. Strong, enduring values equip Savage Leaders with the internal compass they need to build and demonstrate the other mindsets and skillsets in this book.

While there are no right or wrong values, many Savage Leaders have high levels of integrity and honesty. But the key is not to take those as your own—unless you truly connect with them. The key is for you to establish what your values are, apply them consistently, and avoid any temptation to deviate from them in search of short cuts and easy wins. For example, a leader who champions a "customers first" mantra will avoid pressures to trim product or service quality in search of greater profits. Adhering to customer centricity demonstrates to your team that you stay strong in the face of pressure while yielding long-term loyalty from customers.

Once you have your values, it's important that your team and the people you lead know them. Then you have to live up to them. A leader who champions and glowingly refers to their values but fails to use them appears inauthentic. Worse yet, their team will label them a hypocrite, and they will lose their respect. From there, it's a straight line to disengagement and underperformance.

Savage Leaders recognize, embrace, and use their values to guide them in their personal and professional lives.

FIND WHAT MATTERS

Values have always played a crucial role in my life. From regular reminders during childhood from my mom about "being a leader" to my dad talking about the importance of "being fair" and "honest," my values have always been front and center.

While childhood provided a set of values that have served me well, other professional experiences have uncovered more.

In 2007, my priorities became crystal clear while living on a beach outpost in the south of Brazil. My high school friend, Hans and I hatched a plan to escape from corporate America and to follow the road less travelled by starting a business. For him it was escaping the 100-hour weeks at Sullivan & Cromwell, a leading global law firm, where he engaged in soul-sucking work that choked back his ability to pursue his multitude of outside interests.

For me, it was first and foremost driven by a need for creative expression. It also allowed me to combine my love for travel and learning new cultures while immersing and exposing others to them. Most importantly, this opportunity provided an exit ramp from the corporate world to explore the wild west of entrepreneurship.

Hans and I decided to launch Nexus Surf in the fall of 2006 after an early morning surf session at El Porto, a surf break in Manhattan Beach, California. After convincing Melissa (my fiancé at the time—now, my wife) to come along for the adventure, I booked one-way flights to Brazil and put our furniture into long-term storage.

The long-term vision for Nexus Surf was to create the Club Med for action sports. Upon launch however, our focus was creating vacation packages for tourists from the United States to visit Florianopolis, Brazil. Tourists would surf crystal blue waters, enjoy the serene nature and spectacular topography, explore world-class nightlife, and meet the wonderful and vibrant people, food, and culture of Brazil.

My time in Brazil, both as an entrepreneurial and enriching life experience, was one of the most special times of my life.

Each day presented something new and unique. A day trip to scout out the area with our guides João and Xandinho. Taking our first clients to a secluded surf spot in a rickety, wooden boat piloted by local fishermen that almost turned disastrous as a vicious storm blew in after we pulled back into shore. Learning to speak Portuguese while immersing myself in the Brazilian culture.

Beyond the ups and downs of launching a business on foreign soil (which wasn't easy), the biggest lesson I learned came from spending every day and enjoying every meal with Melissa. We discovered favorite haunts and cooked in an ill-equipped vacation rental. Somehow, we managed to make semi-exotic stir-fry's, BBQ chicken pizzas, and traditional barbequed meats using an array of random utensils and a large stone oven on our back patio.

It didn't hit me at the time, but years later when I reflected on what was most important to me in my life, I realized how much I valued freedom of time and space and being present with the people closest to me.

Family and independence became two values that sit at the top of my current value system. Knowing this, has helped guide all of my decisions from starting an executive coaching and training company, to how I build and structure my days now that I'm a father of two boys, to the kinds of clients and projects I take on.

Every decision I face, I ask how it will affect my independence, ability to spend time with my family, and the opportunities I will have to be there for the big moments in my boys' lives. These values play a big role in why I continue playing the entrepreneur game—despite its unpredictability and uncertainty. I willingly embrace the risks that come with this career path for the independence it gives me. I say no to the allure of a big job at a corporate behemoth with just two weeks of vacation, a buzzing phone on nights and weekends, business trips conflicting with my sons' birthdays, and other sacrifices that go along with taking the safe route. While that road would guarantee a certain level of financial success, it would also directly violate my values.

When we violate our values, no one wins.

Key Takeaway

At the core of the Savage Leader, lies a solid bedrock of values that inspire, ground, and remind them of what matters the most in their lives. No matter the temptation or allure of shiny objects, or external pressures, Savage Leaders never deviate from their values.

Having defined values that are authentic to you can act as a beacon and source of motivation through the turbulence you will likely face. You can draw strength and clarity from your values, using them to overcome fear and uncertainty, and to ensure your decisions stay aligned with who you are, who you want to be, and how you want to show up.

Being connected to your values can also remind you that you are guided by something that transcends the ups and downs of a moment and ensures progress toward your long-term goals.

Savage Leaders have a concrete set of values that anchor them to what matters most and to ensure they stay on track in good times and bad.

REVISIT YOUR VALUES REGULARLY

Many people talk about a seminal moment in their lives that forged their purpose and set of values. Browse any bestseller list and you will find a deluge of books that share the author's personal story resulting in a life pivot to focus their energy on making a difference and doing something that matters.

For most people though, values aren't established through a singular moment. Instead, it's a series of experiences and influences in their lives.

So where do our values come from? For many of us, it's our families. According to child and family therapist, Dana Upton, values are first instilled in us from our parents. "There is something called 'intergenerational transmission', that explains how our parents influence us, our perspectives, actions, and outlook through their actions and stories they tell us," said Dana, during our phone conversation. "Of course, genetics play a part and even the experiences you have in utero can help shape you."

According to Dana, over time, we also develop values through experiences, the good and bad. Achieving a resounding success will reinforce values like hard work, overcoming challenges, and perseverance. People who have gone through trying experiences, who have learned to deal with their suffering, and who can acknowledge their success in having made it through, often develop strong, enduring values as a result.

As Dana notes, values also stem from experiencing loss or grief. Typically, our priorities shift after losing something—our loved ones, our careers, or even tangible possessions that make us feel secure and safe like a house. Our values can also come from religion, peers, heroes, and external influences like news and social media.

And they can change as we get older. Time and different experiences can create shifts. "People think that their values are x, y, and z because of how they were raised," Dana told me. "When I challenge them, they recognize that those values aren't congruent any more with their lives. They learn how to challenge their own value systems and priorities to see what changes they want to make that work in their lives today."

Change doesn't happen overnight, cautions Dana. It takes time and effort. As Dana said, "When you have a lifetime of engrained perspectives, it takes time to acknowledge what those values are, and assess how you want to shift, prioritize, add new values, and possibly get rid of some old ones that no longer serve you."

It's critical for us to revisit our values, especially after significant changes and pivotal moments or milestones in our lives. Annual goal setting is a great time to re-examine your values, assess whether or not they still fit in your life and career, and adjust them to achieve greater alignment with your internal motives and beliefs.

Key Takeaway

Our values get forged in many ways—from genetics, our childhood, through good and bad experiences, religion, peers, heroes, and our families. Values, while deeply engrained in both your conscious and subconscious, can change after a trying period of time, experiences, through personal development, or after self-reflection.

Recognizing if your values have changed, requires intentional, deep reflection. Meditation and journaling are two pathways to uncover new values.

Savage Leaders acknowledge their values can shift and intentionally reflect on changes before incorporating any into their lives and careers.

USE YOUR VALUES AS A GUIDE

Values show up in peoples' lives and, by extension, in their organizations in different ways. For Kurt Kaufer, co-founder of Brown Bear Digital (now Ad Results Media), he created a company partly to champion his personal values.

Kurt grew up as a typical kid going to school and playing youth sports in New Jersey. His values were forged by his family and community, who nurtured him. "My values were born out of my childhood," Kurt told me during our interview. "I learned the importance of empathy, the golden rule to 'treat others the way you want to be treated', and that there is a right and wrong way to treat people."

Kurt's childhood experiences and those people closest to him played an impactful role in shaping his values. He recounted many instances and conversations that taught him the importance of being thoughtful about others and their points-of-view and the importance of self-reflection. Those deep and meaningful experiences and conversations became the pillars of Kurt's value set.

Kurt faced a few material challenges during his childhood. Those experiences profoundly impacted him. "It's through the challenges, suffering, or other forms of strife that we dig deep to see who we are and who we want to be," Kurt said.

After graduating from the University of Massachusetts at Amherst, Kurt enjoyed early career success. Despite his achievements, his work didn't lead to happiness. In our conversation, he referenced *The Second Mountain* by David Brooks. It's a book which explores what it takes to lead a meaningful life. "It [the book] articulates my journey very well," he said.

"The first mountain is wrapped up in individualism. Success comes from achieving professional goals, personal progression, getting paid well, etc.," he said in reflecting on the first part of his career.

"After many wins professionally, I was realizing there was a second mountain to climb," he explained. "The second mountain for me came in the form of creating a vehicle where I could create more personal connections but as a mentor and leader, where I serve a community [my employees] in a way that grows them personally and professionally."

For Kurt, starting a company provided an opportunity to climb this second mountain while aligning with his personal values and capturing a marketplace opportunity. "One of the reasons for starting the company was to create a system to spread those values even more," said Kurt.

Kurt, along with fellow partners Michael Kropko and Steven Shanks, launched Brown Bear Digital as a values-driven marketing agency. The company became an extension of Kurt's personal values as well as those of his founding team. It also became a vehicle for sharing and championing values like empathy, fairness and the "golden rule" with his employees, clients, and anyone who interacts with the brand.

Brown Bear Digital has become Kurt's way of taking what his childhood experiences taught him, recognizing the positive impact it had on his life, and passing it along to those in his professional sphere.

"Before we even had a company, I had spent years thinking about how things should be done," he explained, and then Kurt built the company with that in mind. The importance of empathy, integrity, freedom, accountability, gratitude, and transparency became the value pillars of Brown Bear Digital.

Values also play a key role in the day-to-day company operations. As Kurt said, "Values provide a north star in my life. When tough questions come up, I lean on that system to guide me."

Kurt also applies his values when deciding which clients to work with. "We will turn clients down if the same level of respect is not reciprocated," he explained, and he often brings his wife and son into the picture. "Would they be proud of me? Would I want them to act in this way?" he'll ask himself.

In addition to positively impacting employees and clients, Brown Bear Digital has enjoyed even greater success. His firm, which merged with a Houston-based agency to form Ad Results Media, has become the world's leading audio and podcast agency. Kurt also credits the strong, consistent values engrained in the company's culture as helping to recruit top talent while growing and scaling the company. "Our performance is a result of values," noted Kurt. "If you are good to people, it will resonate."

Ultimately, Ad Results Media allows Kurt to fulfill his goal of making a profound impact on his employees through an enduring set of values. As Kurt said, "Knowing that if they decide to leave Ad Results one day, they can look back and realize that working here was one of the best decisions of their life because it prepared them for success and happiness thereafter. I realized that this was my purpose. This was my second mountain."

As Kurt reflected on the importance of his values, he reminded me about where we find our values. "Values aren't found from reading books or listening to a podcast by Tim Ferriss," he said. "Traits have to live inside you and you need to find a way to explore and experience them. It's critical to find that catalyst that brings it out in you. It's about what is true to each of us and makes us feel good as a person."

Key Takeaway

Values are a powerful guide and anchor for you as a leader. They can also be a catalyst for change, and your organization can act as a vehicle to champion values in the marketplace. Values provide purpose and offer direction in good times and in challenging market conditions. They also can help you attract and engage top talent, inform your decision-making, and provide a guide for how you engage with and serve your customers.

Savage Leaders use their values to guide them and look for opportunities to thread them into their teams and organizations to create enduring value.

BE TRUE TO YOUR VALUES

Evan Mendelsohn had a great job with strong long-term prospects as an associate at the law firm, Sheppard Mullin before his career took an unexpected detour in the entrepreneur lane.

Growing up in Redding, a small city in Northeast California, Evan's dad was a doctor and his mom was a nurse. Evan figured he'd follow a tried-and-true path for job security too. He graduated from UC San Diego before earning a joint law degree and Master of Business Administration from the University of Southern California.

Working as a transactional law attorney who served many of the world's most successful companies, Evan was on the safe route, but he felt unfulfilled. "Even though I was paid well at my law firm, I just couldn't find excitement in what I was doing there," he told me. "I believe you should be excited by your job."

Evan has always valued having fun—it's imbued in everything he does. In college, he and his future business partner, Nick Morton would go above and beyond throwing themed parties with elaborate costumes. People loved attending Evan and Nick's parties as much as the guys loved throwing them.

While still toiling in his law firm gig, Evan, while talking with Nick, noticed there were limited options to buy themed clothing. The "fun apparel industry," as Evan calls it, was largely untapped and without any established brands in that space. In particular, Evan and Nick noticed a large trend around ugly Christmas sweater parties that was largely ignored by existing brands.

It wasn't long before ugly Christmas sweaters became the genesis of Evan and Nick's e-commerce company, Tipsy Elves. Using nights and weekends to get it off the ground, Evan found a way to connect his personal value of fun with the excitement of entrepreneurship.

After a successful first season in 2011, the duo made the bold move to quit their day jobs to work on Tipsy Elves full-time. Making the jump was scary given the stability of Evan's job. The skeptical opinions of his colleagues and the nerves that his parents felt for him making such a big transition didn't help, but Evan vowed to stay true to himself. Trusting his gut, Evan went for it.

It was a great decision. It has allowed Evan to connect his passion and value of fun with a successful business endeavor. "Tipsy Elves is a reflection of mine and Nick's most authentic selves," Evan reflected in our phone conversation. The sense of authenticity, he explained, comes from letting out their inner child and from being carefree and having fun. "It goes against what we were doing in our corporate jobs," he continued. "Tipsy Elves allows us to free our inner child on a day-to-day basis which reflects itself within the business."

Having fun has become a core tenet of Tipsy Elves and Evan has stayed involved in hiring to maintain a consistent culture focused on having fun. The result is a work environment that is fun and productive. "Our employees are more productive when they are having as much fun as Nick and I are having," he said.

Fun permeates everything Evan and Nick do at Tipsy Elves; from the products they make to the content they post on social media.

Tipsy Elves has enjoyed strong growth since its inception. Through hard work, and a lot of fun, Evan and Nick earned a spot on ABC's television show, *Shark Tank* in 2013, which led to an investment and partnership with Robert Herjavec. Over time, Tipsy Elves has expanded from a laser focus on ugly Christmas sweaters to "Fun clothing and outfits for every holiday" including clothing for the Fourth of July, St. Patrick's Day, and even ski outfits.

As his company continues to grow and evolve, Evan stays true to his desire and value to have fun in everything he does. "You need to enjoy your work," he said. "For me, that meant building a business from scratch that keeps me young at heart and brings smiles to our customers faces."

Key Takeaway

Many of us have values that would often lead us to the road less travelled. Sometimes, we don't take it. Other times, we fail to stay on it but have the confidence and unwavering faith in our values. Do not allow others to influence, shift, and water down what you believe in or change the direction you follow.

If you are stuck doing soul-sucking work to make a buck but value doing good for your community, fight the gravitational pull of colleagues to break away. Align with and express your values. Ignore what others say, realizing that many people are too scared to accept what they value most and lead a values-centric life. No matter what position you hold, you can always find ways to live your values.

Savage Leaders stay true to their values and find ways to express them in their lives and careers.

THE CHALLENGE: PUT IT INTO PRACTICE

Take a few moments to reflect on what matters most in your life. Jot down a list of words that reflect your values and what's most important to you. Some of the most common values that I've heard include: faith, family, security, financial success, independence, fairness, compassion, justice, honesty, truth, and transparency. This isn't an exhaustive list, so pick values that strongly resonate for you.

If you already have an established set of values, add new ones that come up and narrow the combined list to three to five. Then look for opportunities to live them more fully. Connect your values to the mission of your team or company to cultivate purpose and greater meaning. Find more ways to express your values through volunteer work and in your personal life.

Aligning values with your actions will support your success and also yield greater satisfaction and happiness in your life.

SAVAGE PRINCIPLE #2
ADAPT BEST PRACTICES FOR AUTHENTICITY

"There must be a certain amount of imitation, copying, in outward technique, but when there is inward, psychological imitation surely we cease to be creative."

Jiddu Krishnamurti

Most leadership books and inspirational keynotes leave us with the same message: do exactly what the author or speaker did and we will achieve the same (incredible) results.

Except, we are unique.

Each of us has a different combination of strengths, experiences, values, and beliefs. Why should we use a copy and paste method of applying other people's best practices to our own lives—that all too often, leave us feeling like failures when we come up short? The adulation of world-changing entrepreneurs such as Jeff Bezos, Elon Musk, Steve Jobs, and Richard Branson further reinforces us to be zombie-like followers of methods that work for very unique individuals.

For many rabid consumers of leadership gospels, we're left in a trance of conflicting methods and techniques to resolve conflict, motivate our teams, manage our time, figure out how to succeed, or level-up on a host of other business and leadership topics. We are essentially left with two choices: choose one method and follow it blindly, even if that means off a cliff, or mix and match techniques and methods that might conflict and not deliver the desired results.

Either choice is potentially hazardous, if applied blindly and without adapting best practices to our individual styles, preferences, and unique situations.

Fortunately, Savage Leaders know how to take best practices and adapt them to fit their individual styles and strengths, and specific situations.

ALLOW FLEXIBILITY IN EXECUTING A LEADERSHIP DECREE

Years ago, I observed a CEO passionately dictate to his entire organization that, "Everyone must sell!" Sales had been crucial to his success as an entrepreneur, so he assumed that was also the case for the rest of the team. But his stern mandate led to confusion and concern among the delivery and operations teams, who didn't see big-game hunting as part of their jobs.

Worse yet, an overemphasis on selling for people who didn't have sales as part of their role, led to lower productivity, awkward sales conversations led by members of the delivery team to potential clients, and lower engagement across the company.

What the CEO failed to convey, or perhaps should have said, was "Everyone needs to support sales for our company, and I'll empower each of you to find the best way to do so." This would have empowered his team to adapt the request based on their individual styles, roles, and strengths. For example, those who possessed competitive strengths could have created a scoreboard of leads, deals closed, and revenue booked and compared it with others in the company—making it a game and challenge.

For others on the team who may have been driven by process, they could have sought ways for the company to implement a more effective sales process. Maybe they would have uncovered new ways for everyone to personally and authentically sell.

The point is we are all different. Following directives literally can lead to a lack of execution and a lower level of employee engagement.

Savage Leaders focus on supporting, encouraging, and driving authentic practices and behaviors—both for themselves and for everyone on their teams.

Key Takeaway

Be careful not to dictate a singular path to deliver on your vision and mission for the company or the strategy to achieve it. Provide room for your team to individualize organizational directives, supporting them to also use their unique sets of values and strengths.

If you aren't in a formal leadership role, you can also apply this by providing flexibility when you make a request of colleagues and team members. Give them space and trust them to complete the task in their own preferred style.

Savage Leaders recognize the uniqueness of individual team members, allowing them to customize their approaches to leverage their unique styles and strengths.

TAILOR BEST PRACTICES FOR FIT

Elon Musk is well known as a swashbuckling risk-taker able to take on the launch of multiple companies simultaneously. Musk credits what he calls "batching" or "always multi-tasking." For instance, he conducts business on his phone during meetings and sends emails while he checks invoices. Musk is also known to send work-related texts with his children on his lap, though the merits of that are up for debate.

Maybe these practices work for Musk, but for most of us, the cognitive overload and costs of multi-tasking often leads to decreased performance, longer time to complete tasks, and potential disasters. So just because Musk does this, it doesn't mean we should.

I was coaching a woman who tried adopting a similar Musk-like multi-tasking approach. It was her solution to getting through the seemingly impossible task list that came with her promotion and new role. She saw conference calls as opportunities to catch-up on customer emails or for finishing documents that she'd zap to customers.

She learned quickly that while doing all this work, she could only half-listen on the calls. Inevitably, she would miss key details and follow-up items while sending out deliverables to customers with obvious mistakes that she normally would have caught, if she was paying full attention.

Over time, she tailored batching to her own style which meant pairing similar tasks requiring limited brainpower like cleaning up her desk or organizing her email inbox with a low-cognition task like listening to a podcast. This allowed her to regain time in her day while also performing at her well-established level—which earned her the promotion in the first place.

One size doesn't fit all when it comes to applying best practices. Just because something works for the leaders in one field, doesn't mean it will work for everyone. I coached a group of executives, and I mentioned how Warren Buffet spends 80 percent of his time reading and researching. The conversation quickly devolved into a debate about why Buffet's best practice wouldn't work for the executives. First, Buffet's role at Berkshire Hathaway is to uncover new opportunities, future trends, and investment opportunities. The executives I coached had a broader set of responsibilities.

Second, while everyone agreed with the importance of ongoing learning, each executive goes about it differently. One executive carves out time each weekend to read a book on a new topic. Another one creates a summer reading list that he knocks out during his long vacation and over the holidays. One CEO focuses on experiential learning (learn by doing) and testing out new leadership, learning, and business methods in bite-size ways during his day.

Whose practice was the best? Everyone's. Best practices are very useful. It's helpful to learn what works for other people, but only when we adapt those practices to fit our unique situations, styles, and preferences.

This goes for how we weave them into our organizations and teams too. Similarly, I've observed many executives build and execute a new strategy based on industry best practices. These executives conducted exhaustive research to capture and apply what other successful executives had used. The problem was that these best practices were treated like gospel. Different industries have different best practices, and often within industries, best practices differ from company to company. Instead of adopting best practices as they were, the executives failed to see the opportunities to individualize the best practices based on their organization's strengths, and the particular leaders, their teams, and the culture.

The most successful leaders I've worked with and coached were those who didn't lift best practices and directly apply them. Rather, those leaders tailored each practice to fit their teams, culture, and organization. For example, Lisa, the CEO of a leading manufacturer, wanted to bring greater agility and innovation to her organization. She studied how technology companies used daily stand-up meetings to drive projects to completion. In the technology world, product cycles are shorter than in manufacturing, which needs more time to design, develop, and test. Lisa knew daily meetings wouldn't give her team enough time to make progress, but she wanted to bring them together more regularly for updates and troubleshooting. Instead of holding daily meetings, Lisa experimented with twice-weekly.

Lisa also switched the long-established hierarchical culture that limited input from more junior team members, to rotating roles in meetings so everyone on the team offered their ideas and feedback.

The result was greater innovation, new product ideas, and better collaboration across groups that rarely interacted.

Key Takeaway

Avoid the temptation to directly mirror the methods of thought leaders, mentors, and your idols. Instead consider, filter, adapt, and transform best practices into authentic practices based on *your* individual values, beliefs, strengths, experiences, and organization.

This allows you to use the practices more often, and will make them feel more natural. This in turn means you'll also apply them with greater confidence. More confidence will change the way you show up and allow you to lead with greater impact.

Savage Leaders constantly seek out new methods to improve their performance and adapt best practices to fit their unique styles and strengths. They demonstrate Savage Practices, not copycat best practices.

THE CHALLENGE: PUT IT INTO PRACTICE

The next time you read a book, watch a TED Talk, or listen to a podcast focused on personal or professional development, take a few minutes to reflect afterwards. Ask and answer the following questions:

- Which lessons or tips will offer the biggest benefit to my life and career?
- What would be the benefit(s) of applying them?
- Which best practices fit my style and strengths?
- How do I need to adapt each of the tips to fit me, so I have the confidence to apply them?
- Which one(s) am I willing to commit to trying next week?

Next, write down the tips you will apply and by when. Be sure to log a reminder in your calendar so you remember to take action. Also, build in accountability by sharing what you are going to do with a friend or colleague. Report back on how it went and what you can do next time to improve the impact and results.

FORGE UNBREAKABLE BONDS WITH YOUR TRIBE

"The most basic and powerful way to connect with another person is to listen. Just listen. Perhaps the most important thing we ever give each other is our attention. A loving silence often has far more power to heal and connect than the most well-intentioned words."

Rachel Naomi Remen

Command and control. That's the approach many leaders continue using despite the fact that it was a model best suited during the industrial revolution when a rigid rules-based approach was critical. In an era requiring agility, collaboration, and fast decision making, command and control fails on many accounts.

Leaders beat the drum for greater productivity and "getting sh*t done," but these leaders often fail to take time out and balance achieving outcomes with developing their teams. This is especially true during trying times such as the 2008 mortgage crisis, and the Coronavirus pandemic. Fear and uncertainty, mixed with a scarcity mindset often drives leaders to intensely focus on outcomes and survival, at all costs. It's a rational approach during tough times, but will hinder medium and long-term success by neglecting individual and team development.

How we accomplish tasks and initiatives is just as important as *what* we accomplish. We need to be aware of how we achieve our goals, and not just bulldoze our way to the outcome. Engaging and empowering our teams along the way will help us drive key wins and meet objectives.

Even the most productive and energetic leaders can't take their organizations on their back and single-handedly make them successful. Enduring success comes by activating the strengths of every member of the organization. Even if you're not in a traditional leadership role, you still have the power to influence, inspire, engage, and connect with everyone on your team.

How we communicate, and our ability to connect with our teams are imperative for our individual and team success. We must connect to engage. Connect to empower. Connect to inspire.

Savage Leaders connect. They forge strong, near unbreakable bonds with their teams that help everyone to win.

BE CURIOUS TO UNCOVER NEW IDEAS AND OPPORTUNITIES

Hollywood producer, Brian Grazer has nurtured curiosity to advance his career and build one of the most successful production houses in the industry. Imagine Entertainment has produced films including *Apollo 13*, and *A Beautiful Mind*, as well as TV shows including *Arrested Development, Empire*, and *Friday Night Lights*.

Brian has used what he calls "Curiosity Conversations" to meet Hollywood power brokers and research the subjects of his groundbreaking films and TV shows. Brian broke into the movie business after overhearing a conversation outside of his apartment window about a job in the legal department at Warner Brothers. Brian landed the gig that included bringing legal documents to actors, producers, and other Hollywood influencers. He insisted on hand delivering every letter, so he could spark conversations with the people who would ultimately change his life.

"I started having what I called curiosity conversations," Brian writes in his book, *A Curious Mind: The Secret to a Bigger Life.* "At first, they were just inside the business... But pretty quickly I realized that I could actually reach out and talk to anyone, in any business that I was curious about."

Brian went on to have conversations with actors, entertainers, titans of industry, heads of state, and anyone who provided a unique take on the world. His Curiosity Conversations created connections and yielded a robust network of contacts.

These conversations worked for two reasons.

First, Brian had the stones to make the ask, even knowing there was a good chance he'd get turned down. That required thick skin and perseverance.

Second, Brian's impetus for these conversations was centered on learning and genuine curiosity—they weren't for commercial gain. He never knew what gem he'd discover from the conversations. Many inspired his later works and provided content for films like *Apollo 13*.

Like Brian, Savage Leaders are inherently curious about the world and people around them. They are curious to learn from everyone with diverse perspectives, and eager to unearth new ideas, access new insights, and gain a better understanding of the people they work with.

I know that for some people, initiating conversations, especially with people they may not know very well, can feel uncomfortable, especially at first. But Savage Leaders do it anyway.

Perhaps more importantly, Savage Leaders put aside their preconceived answers and suggestions when engaging with their team members. They lead with curiosity, genuinely wanting to know what someone has to say. They don't influence conversations and interactions with their biases.

By approaching their teams like this, they lay the groundwork for what's called active listening. For all the managers and higher-ups, this is critical to supporting and developing your teams. Genuine curiosity will help encourage your team members' growth, ensuring you don't direct them in a way that solely serves your goals.

Approaching your team with curiosity and active listening can generate more engaged and empowered employees, who feel compelled to continue growing and developing in ways that align their individual career goals with that of the team and organization.

Key Takeaway

Curiosity is both a mindset and tactic to help us uncover new opportunities as well as to show people that we are truly interested in them—what they have to say, what they think, and who they are as people. Being curious starts with a dose of humility, accepting that other people and ideas are interesting and are worth exploring.

You can practice greater curiosity by asking lots of questions, not just to get an answer or to see how it aligns with your own point of view, but to gain a deeper understanding of different, yet equally valid, ideas. Be open and consider how these conversations can expand your opinion, plan, or ideas, while simultaneously strengthening your bond with the people on your team.

Savage Leaders are curious about the world around them, looking outward for ideas and inspiration, and genuinely engage their teams to help them grow and develop.

REPLACE DIRECTING WITH A FOCUS ON DEVELOPMENT

A few years back, I worked with a Shawn, a leader at a midsize e-commerce company, who felt he inspired his teams and was great at developing them. I was curious, because Shawn's team routinely had low-engagement scores. When I probed why he believed he was great at developing people, Shawn told me, "I delegate tasks to my team and empower them to get the work done."

Indeed, Shawn did trust his team to pick up the tasks he "threw over the wall," but that's as far as he went. He didn't spend time working with his people to help them improve their abilities so they could successfully complete each task and grow in ways that would support regular career promotions.

During our coaching sessions, we reviewed how Shawn conducted his individual and team meetings. He realized he used a command-and-control approach focused on what tasks he needed people to complete and then he left the team to figure out how to execute.

To improve his team's engagement and help them develop their skills, Shawn shifted to weekly 30-minute, one-on-one conversations with each team member. During these meetings, he focused on what each team member hoped to achieve during the week and how that aligned with their longer-term career objectives. Instead of laying out the meeting agenda and weekly priorities, Shawn adopted active listening while asking questions such as, "What are you hoping to learn over the next year that will help you achieve your long-term career goals?" and, "What can I do, and what resources can I provide, to support your learning and development?"

The biggest shift happened when Shawn genuinely started to care and learn about his team members past work and life experiences. This helped him better develop each team member as individuals. Greater understanding of each team member's values and experiences helped Shawn better motivate everyone by framing new projects and tasks in ways that aligned with what mattered most to them.

The new approach resulted in team members who felt both cared about and supported in learning new skills while also ensuring the deadlines critical to Shawn and the team's success were met. A true win-win!

Key Takeaway

The best leaders replace conversations rooted in an old-school, command-and-control structure that was focused on directing, to having interactions that center on the development of their team. This approach has three key benefits. First, it accelerates the growth and performance of team members so that they can learn from their leader's experience, insight, and guidance. Second, teams will feel empowered and will take greater accountability and ownership of their career growth and of tasks and projects. Finally, employee engagement will increase through a greater sense of their leader caring for them and their success—all which leads to lower attrition and higher productivity.

You can try this leadership approach with your direct reports, and colleagues and peers too—this isn't solely a management technique. Be sure to show up for your teammates and find ways to be of service to their individual development by listening, sharing insights, and offering to be a sounding board.

Savage Leaders are curious about exploring the people and the world around them and helping everyone to grow and develop so they meet their full potential (maybe even achieve greatness) too.

BE HUMBLE AND ENGAGE

Savage Leaders aren't concerned with being the smartest person in the room or focused on receiving all the accolades. They understand that to execute at a high level and to make the progress they aspire to, they need help. Savage Leaders know they need to recruit top talent, so they have more time to focus on the responsibilities that they are uniquely qualified to do. This takes humility. It takes the ability to step aside, to let other people succeed, and to ditch the "me first" attitude.

Humility isn't a weakness; it's a strength and more people are recognizing how powerful it is. Take for instance, Navid Alipour, co-founder and managing partner of Analytics Ventures, a venture capital firm based in San Diego focused on artificial intelligence and machine learning. When vetting start-ups for investment opportunities, Navid and his team look for a "CEO who has humility and doesn't have that ego," he told me in our interview. "A good CEO is looking to replace himself in every capacity, which allows them to focus on growth activities like fund raising and building out the leadership team."

Humility offers Savage Leaders a number of benefits. First, it creates space for team members to offer their perspectives and insights in place of deference to the all-knowing person at the top. When a Savage Leader displays humility, it signals to everyone that it is safe for them to take a risk and offer new, potentially game changing ideas and insights. When people fear being mocked, ridiculed, or criticized then they don't speak up.

Second, Savage Leaders with humility empower team members, who know that their contributions matter and make a difference. When people know they're partially responsible for the organization's success, they take greater ownership—especially when leaders acknowledge their valuable contributions.

Finally, when Savage Leaders show humility, it increases their likeability and team members and colleagues' genuinely want to help their leaders succeed.

Key Takeaway

Connecting with your teams and forging strong bonds requires you to be humble. That means acknowledging that you don't have all the answers to every challenge; that you can accept your strengths and shortcomings; that you can and will own up to your mistakes and poor decisions; and that you're willing to learn from your peers and direct reports, and not just leaders and mentors.

Savage Leaders who demonstrate humility help create greater connection with their colleagues, peers, direct reports, and bosses—which contributes to a more engaged workplace.

Savage Leaders use humility to connect and deepen relationships up, down, and laterally within their organizations.

LEAD THROUGH LISTENING

"I listen to my team," is a common phrase I hear leaders say.

Yet how many leaders truly listen? It turns out, most people listen at 25 percent efficiency. Listening requires being present in the moment, having a curiosity to learn, and the humility to accept that they don't have all the answers.

A few years back, I observed a CEO excitedly express his desire for his team to vocalize their perspectives and take ownership of the firm and its success. But when it came time to support this decree with action, the CEO unfortunately affirmed the opposite. As team members chimed in during leadership meetings, I could see the impatience on his face—he wanted to jump in and resume control of the conversation, and he did. By railroading team members, he caused people to withhold their opinions. For those who did share, they spoke in hyper-speed—knowing the clock was ticking and their CEO was about to cut them off at any time.

The meetings failed and it was because of the CEO.

What prevented this CEO from listening? The easy answer was his desire for rapid action. But the deeper answer was that he lacked curiosity to learn and the humility to accept that others might know more than him on a given topic.

In contrast, I observed a CEO of a large public company casually sit back during leadership meetings and listen to all of the perspectives in the room. Not listening to drive consensus, but to ensure team members felt heard and valued and so all perspectives were on the table.

If I walked blindly into that room, I would never have known who the CEO was at first glance. He only punctuated his perspective and direction at the end of each agenda item, opting to give his team the time and space for their contributions.

That was Savage listening.

Key Takeaway

As you engage your team, choke back the desire to assert and influence, and just listen. Hear what is being said and what isn't. Watch for body language including posture, facial expressions, and gestures—those are keys to help us better understand people and what they're thinking and feeling. Listening can help you learn, engage more deeply, and empower your colleagues.

Savage Leaders are active listeners who provide time and space for others to contribute.

USE QUESTIONS TO CREATE NEW POSSIBILITIES

Want to really engage your team and forge strong bonds? Don't just listen, ask powerful, possibility-evoking questions. Questions are more important than ever given the amount of information we are exposed to every day. In his book, *A More Beautiful Question: The Power of Inquiry to Spark Breakthrough Ideas,* author Warren Berger writes that the value of questions is increasing and the value of answers is dropping to zero due to the continued accumulation of data, insights, and answers online and with Google at our fingertips and Alexa at the ready.

Unfortunately, our current school systems and default parenting methods provide negative reinforcement to kids' insatiable appetite to ask questions. According to the Right Question Institute, "Students typically hit their question-asking peak around the age of 4 and their question asking dramatically declines shortly after they enter the classroom." This is due partly to students being rewarded for responding with the "right" answer, not for asking open-ended, exploratory questions.

If our early academic experience discourages asking questions, how can leaders ask more and better questions? First, Savage Leaders set the tone by defaulting to asking questions even when their instinct is to jump in with answers. Instead of quickly assessing or judging a team member's proposal or idea, Savage

Leaders will ask questions like "What assumptions underlie your recommendation?" or, "What is the range of possible outcomes with your suggestion?"

Second, Savage Leaders will avoid asking closed questions that require yes or no responses, and will use open-ended questions. This means that instead of asking "Will this approach work?" or, "Do you have what you need to be successful?" Savage Leaders will ask "What assumptions are we making with this approach?" or, "What other tools and resources can I provide to ensure your success?"

Asking open-ended questions that start with "what" and "how" requires intention, time, curiosity, humility, and active listening—but if you've embraced the other sections in this chapter, this should be easy.

Key Takeaway

Questions are a powerful tool to uncover new possibilities and ideas, and help Savage Leaders deeply engage with their team members. The best questions are "open" and aren't intended to drive an agenda like a courtroom attorney. Questions have no an agenda or destination.

During your next meeting, try asking more open-ended questions to spur more innovation and new ideas, and to accelerate your team's professional growth.

Savage Leaders spend more time asking rather than answering questions and carve out time for thought-provoking ones as a part of regular meetings—not just in brainstorming sessions.

THE CHALLENGE: PUT IT INTO ACTION

Connecting with your colleagues in a meaningful way requires a mindset of curiosity and humility along with cultivating the skills of active listening and posing open-ended questions. Before the next meeting with a colleague, ask yourself one or more of the following questions:

- What is one thing I want to learn more about?

- What experiences or skills does my colleague/team member possess that I would like to better understand?
- What is one thing I can do to ensure I will listen first and talk second?
- What are a few open-ended questions I can ask that pertain to the meeting agenda?

Be sure to also try these suggestions in your personal life with your spouse, significant other, children, and friends. Remember, Savage Leaders lead in all areas of their lives. Try to forge stronger bonds with the people around you and watch what new insights and discoveries you glean about the people closest to you. You'll be surprised and amazed at how you'll begin connecting in new and different (and most likely stronger) ways.

COMMIT TO LIFELONG LEARNING AND GROWTH

"My training is never complete."

Navy SEAL Ethos

With rapid change as the new normal, Savage Leaders must accelerate the pace of their learning, if they're to keep up. They can't wait for their companies or a government training program to teach them the skills they'll need to survive and thrive in an uncertain future.

Leaders who are stagnant and don't constantly sharpen their skills and gain new knowledge will quickly find themselves outflanked by their more ambitious, learning-oriented colleagues. Promotions will take longer and will be harder to achieve. New, innovative ideas will happen less frequently and more inconsistently. Excitement, interest, and focus will wane.

We live in a hectic world that pulls us in multiple directions. With everyone and everything vying for our time and attention, it can be tough to carve out time for ongoing learning and growth. But for those people who do, opportunities, potentials, and possibilities for what they can achieve in their careers, increase exponentially.

Savage Leaders embrace their development with vigor, dedication, and focus. They understand that knowledge and information are the gateways to greatness. They take their learning upon themselves, and they build personalized ongoing, constantly evolving development plans. Then they commit to taking action to close any and all skill gaps.

TEACH YOURSELF THE SKILLS YOU NEED TO THRIVE

Like many first-time CEOs, Tom Spengler, founder of the technology company Granicus, knew he needed more knowledge and enhanced skills to build and scale his team and organization.

Tom started Granicus in 1999, after a stint at Accenture. While he had been a successful college athlete, had excelled at Accenture, and considered himself a natural leader in many aspects of his life, Tom was new to the startup world and to being a CEO.

If his company was to succeed, he had to grow and develop, so Tom became an avid reader. As he told me during our conversation, "I would read one book per week, books about leadership and general business books."

Every book gave Tom some new insight, inspiration, or knowledge that he applied directly to his company, his strategy for growth, his leadership style, or how he inspired his team. "The book, *Good to Great* inspired me to build a great company," noted Tom, "while the book, *Crossing the Chasm*, made me realize we needed to focus on a small niche opportunity versus trying to go after the largest opportunity possible."

Tom also read books for practical tips. "*Solution Selling* was the core to my sales framework and how we thought about our buyers," he said.

It's easy to forget the lessons we learn from a book once we close the back cover. To help Tom remember and maximize what he learned, he took detailed notes while reading. He went further by creating personalized Cliff Notes for each book that contained the strategies, tips, and tactics that resonated with him.

These became quick and easy reference guides that Tom could grab whenever he needed them. For example, after reading *Strategic Selling* by Robert B. Miller, Tom created grids highlighting the needs of each type of buyer, as well as how to achieve wins with each.

For Michael Porter's, *Competitive Advantage*, a dense book for any reader, it took Tom six months to complete. His notes consisted of distilling what could be a theoretical, MBA program into practical tips that he could apply directly to his business. In the section about competitive differentiation, he wrote, "Granicus Note - This is a big goal of customer advocacy to get our clients to realize the full value of our solution." Tom then listed five ways to achieve it for integration into their strategy at the time.

Tom's commitment to reading and applying the lessons he picked up helped him to grow and eventually sell Granicus in 2014. Reading has continued to be critical to Tom's success as his career has shifted. He's gone from mentoring and advising other startups and executives to assuming leadership roles at fast growing start-ups. He is currently the Executive Chairman of PrimeGov, a company dedicated to unlocking the potential of municipal governments through technology, to promoting transparency to empower citizens, and to fostering civic engagement.

No matter the position or role that Tom finds himself in, he knows that books can help him gain invaluable skills and knowledge that will propel him on his path to greatness. "It is always on my annual goals list," he said.

Key Takeaway

Learning is critical at all career levels—from the entry level to middle manager to the entrepreneur to the executive. By embracing ongoing learning, it provides a proven pathway to help you elevate into new, unfamiliar roles. It can also pave the path to greater career growth and future promotions. Continuous learning can help you to close key skill gaps, while inspiring you to apply what you learn to your company or in your role.

Books are a rich resource of knowledge and information. Do more than check books off your reading list. Read to learn and get ahead, but be sure to also write down what you learned and commit to applying it in your life and business.

Savage Leaders take the extra step to distill insight from a variety of sources, codify it, and apply it immediately.

SURROUND YOURSELF WITH TOP PERFORMERS TO PUSH YOU HIGHER

Surrounding yourself with "A" level talent is another key to ongoing learning and development.

I spoke with a current NBA player, who I'll call "Michael" (not his real name). Michael came out of high school as a white-hot prospect and had his pick of top NCAA basketball programs. Rather than choose a school where he would be the singular talent, he committed to one with a stacked roster of future NBA players.

Being surrounded by fellow stars forced Michael to step up his game and prevented him from coasting, during his freshman year—a year that could have easily been a year of inflated stats. During his freshman year, Michael developed a well-rounded skillset that complemented the talents of his teammates. All of this prepared him to succeed as a 19-year-old rookie playing for a playoff-caliber team.

"It [playing with top talent] helped me in ways I couldn't imagine," Michael told me during our conversation. "In high school, I always had the ball in my hand, and I was the main focus on every team I was on. When I got to college, it taught me the little things that I need to do in the NBA now. On my current team, we have two established All-Stars and a lot of veterans. The things I was doing in college—I was catching and shooting, knocking down shots, moving within the offense to try to set people up—that's all that I have to do right now. My team doesn't need me to come in right now and average 20, 25 [points per game]. I have to prove that I can do that. College taught me to do the little things like catch and shoot, cover great players, and there was a lot of light in that."

Playing for a college team with a stacked roster forced Michael to round out his game and enabled him to be ready when he took the next step to the NBA. Doing so has paid dividends and helped him right out of the gate. He has a bright future in the pros, and that's in part to a constant focus on growth and learning.

Key Takeaway

Successful leaders surround themselves with high achievers who have ambitious goals regardless of their role. As author and speaker, Jim Rohn said, "You are the average of the five people you spend the most time with." This applies to athletes, entrepreneurs, and successful people in any field.

Friends with middling goals will fail to challenge and inspire you to get better and achieve greater accomplishments in life. I'm not suggesting smashing the eject button on these friendships, especially if they bring tremendous value to your life. But I encourage you to look for ways to up the time spent with other like-minded, top-caliber talent who will challenge and inspire you to greater heights.

Likewise, working on teams with other top performers will force you to develop a well-rounded skill set. No one does it all. Not everyone has the ability to set the vision, lead team meetings, or facilitate brainstorming sessions. A Savage Leader may not always get designated as the official leader, running meetings and managing a project or team. That's okay. Everyone is important and Savage Leaders know this.

They seek other roles and opportunities such as leading critical market research, creating insightful and easy to consume deliverables, and building plans to roll out a new strategy within their organization. In these positions, Savage Leaders still seek to learn, grow, and advance their skills.

No matter your role, there's a lot to learn.

Savage Leaders surround themselves with high achievers to inspire them and don't fear being on teams of top performers—they see those as rich with learning opportunities.

USE LEARNING TO MAKE CAREER PIVOTS

PGA golfer, Trevor Murphy grew up in a ski racing family in Vermont. At the age of two, he took to the slopes. "Skiing was my passion and I started racing pretty young," he said when we spoke. Given his early promise on the snow, Trevor's parents sent him to Burke Mountain Academy, the premier skiing academy and boarding school for aspiring Olympic skiers. The academy has produced the most Olympians including three-time Olympic medalist Mikaela Shiffrin, one of the prominent faces of the 2018 Olympics.

Trevor's promise was realized quickly—he was among the top three Americans in his age group and competed in the World Juniors event along with fellow Americans and ski legends including Lindsey Vonn and Julia Mancuso.

After achieving early success, Trevor suffered a devastating injury. He tore his ACL while skiing during his junior year of high school and quit racing.

Whereas this could have left anyone floundering, trying to find their next path, Trevor already had a back-up plan—though he didn't realize it at the time. "I started playing golf late at the age of 13 and fell in love with the game," he recalled. "Most summers from June to August, I would play every day. I remember turning down a camp to play golf. I was a teenager and I was a little burnt out."

While most future PGA pros start playing at an early age, Trevor bucked the trend by breaking in despite his late start. "I grew up playing a muni course in Vermont versus kids who grew up playing golf like I grew up skiing."

Rather than let his late start and growing up in Vermont be a detriment, Trevor found his advantages. "One benefit [of starting late] was that I was super passionate about it when I was coming into it versus some of the other kids who were burnt out."

His time at the ski academy also served him well—he developed a keen ability to persevere during tough periods. "The ski academy was a big commitment and going there was intense," he said. "The whole school would be doing a workout, then going to school, and then going up on the hill, then tuning skis, and then studying. It was much harder than college. If you can get through it at that age, you can do anything."

During his junior year of high school, one of Trevor's friends was attempting to qualify for a U.S. Junior golf event in the summer. "I went with him and ended up winning the qualifier," he said. From there Trevor played in the U.S. Juniors in San Antonio. It was his first tournament, and he played with Kevin Kisner (25th on the PGA leaderboard at the time of writing this) in his first two rounds.

From there, Trevor's been on the PGA path.

One of the keys to his successful pivot from skiing to golf was his desire to learn and get better, paired with an acute self-awareness. Trevor knew he started very late compared to most pros, but he didn't let that hold him back. "It's important to be eager to learn and to hear new things," he said. "I ask a lot of questions and try not to be annoying."

Trevor would ask everyone he met who was involved with the game about how to approach it and what to do in specific situations. Building on the desire to learn and constantly get better, Trevor uses greater self-awareness as a tool to guide his growth and development. "Just be self-aware," he said while also being mindful of any tendencies toward being hypercritical. "I can be a little critical of myself, like a perfectionist. I can play a good round and guys will say, 'you hit it well.' If I hit two bad shots, it just overrides the good shots that I hit. That could be negative, but it can also be positive."

Trevor leverages the self-awareness and puts it into action by using a number of tools to improve his game. Specifically, he turns to the vast array of information online to support his success. "I am always on YouTube," he told me. "I love hearing different golf theories and I am always trying to get that edge."

As a golfer who competes without a swing coach, online tools are a trove of insight for Trevor to use so he continually improves. Trevor has used the constant hunt for new knowledge and tips to fuel his successful golf career.

Key Takeaway

You can pivot into new roles and careers, if you have an intense desire to learn and get better. Use self-awareness to guide how you need to improve, and commit to learning via multiple modalities. If you seek change in your life, dial-up your learning efforts to close any knowledge and skill gaps. Yes, pivoting or growing can strike fear—anything uncertain will. But Savage Leaders welcome that fear—they know it's a sign that they're evolving toward greatness, so they double-down on learning to ensure they have the skills they need.

Savage Leaders embrace pivots in work and life by tapping their internal drive to learn and put in the work to make the transition.

CREATE A TRIBE OF LEARNERS

At Zovio, an education technology company based in Chandler, Arizona many of the leaders and managers have shelves stocked full of their favorite leadership books. Rather than just collect dust, Phil Dana, former Vice President of Talent Acquisition & HR Operations, advocated for the formation of an informal "Book Club" for executives.

Members selected chapters for their fellow leaders to read or to re-read for a quick refresher. "People will say, 'Go back and re-read *Turn Your Ship Around*,'" he explained during our conversation. Phil also encouraged his team to do the equivalent of "an arms workout day" on a periodic basis. So the team would focus on a specific area of knowledge or leadership to learn more about.

Instituting a book club helped foster an environment of peer-to-peer learning, closed specific knowledge gaps, and translated individual insights into a collective organizational knowledge base that endures today.

Key Takeaway

Learning doesn't have to be a solo mission. It can be shared with your team. It's also a great way to start building some collective organizational knowledge that can live within the company. Make it enduring and sticky by posting snippets of text, personal Cliff Notes, and book recommendations on collaboration tools such as Slack and Dropbox. This ensures the insights go beyond tribal knowledge that can walk out of the building during a time of change.

Savage Leaders constantly hunt for new knowledge and innovations to give them an edge. They ask fellow leaders what podcasts they listen to, their favorite TED Talks, who to follow on Twitter, and books to read on vacation that will inspire and inform. Learn to get ahead by tapping into the knowledge and recommendations from your network.

CULTIVATE SKILLS YOU WILL NEED IN THE FUTURE, NOT JUST NOW

Athletes, like entrepreneurs and business leaders, invest downstream in their development curve to ensure long-term success. They constantly hunt for new tips and training techniques to improve their game—not just the one they're playing now, but the one coming in the future.

Consider Michael Jordan one of the most dominant basketball players over the last 30 years. Do you think he started to learn and develop alternative ways to score after his raw explosiveness had started to fade? The superstar athlete started to layer the turn-around jump shot into his game in the years before his predictable decline.

After dominating in his twenties with superior athleticism, Jordan honed his skill in posting up defenders and mastering a deadly fadeaway jump shot that he used later in his career. "…At the end of his career, Michael transformed himself into one of the best post-up players in the NBA. He was nearly unstoppable because he perfected his bump and fadeaway jump shot," wrote NBA announcer, Hubie Brown on NBA.com.

Despite a radical change in his game, Jordan continued to enjoy enduring success. He led the league in scoring 10 times, and also holds the record for the oldest player (at ages 32, 33, and 34) to lead the league. Learning new skills and adapting his game was crucial to being able to succeed as "Air Jordan" started to play closer to earth.

Key Takeaway

Future proof your company and career by anticipating the skills and knowledge you will need as your career and industry change. Don't put your head in the sand and hope that it will pass. Look forward to assess the skills and knowledge that will be needed not just to survive, but to thrive in the future.

For example, reading, attending seminars, and taking online classes can help you stay on top of industry trends, new management principles, and new tools that are being introduced in the workplace. Also, take time to learn more about new technologies even if they have yet to be widely implemented in your industry. Stay current and knowledgeable by becoming a voracious consumer of content and ideas.

Savage Leaders invest time, money, and effort to grow and adapt to the inevitable changes to come.

THE CHALLENGE: PUT IT INTO ACTION

Take a moment to consider a big goal you have for yourself, your team, or your organization. Then objectively answer the following questions?

- What is one skill (e.g. improve my writing or public speaking) that I need to get better at in order to ensure I achieve my goal?

- What new knowledge do I need to gain to increase the odds of reaching my goal?

- Who can I talk with that would have insight into what I am trying to do?

- What facts or data could I research to help better inform me?

Once you have honestly answered those questions, create a set of learning goals and commit to achieving them in support of your success. Be sure that each goal is specific and also has a timeline to complete. Better yet, partner with a colleague and share your respective goals, then commit to holding one another accountable to achieving each of them.

PRACTICE MENTAL AND PHYSICAL REPS TO WIN WHEN IT COUNTS

"Most of our waking hours, we feel as though we're in a trench on the front lines with bullets whizzing past our heads. Through 20 minutes of consistent meditation, I can become the commander, looking out at the battlefield from a hilltop."

Tim Ferriss

Success requires more than focus and effort in the moment; it commands mental and physical preparation too.

Many leaders mistakenly think they can show up and perform without prior mental or physical repetitions. After an unsuccessful investor presentation, sales pitch, performance review, or even team meeting, many leaders will vow to get better next time. But what does that mean? What gets done? What gets practiced and perfected? How does that happen?

It's not enough to say, "I'll do better next time" without actually doing anything differently.

Savage Leaders recognize that performing in the moment requires a lot of hard work in advance. Think rehearsing, recording, and reviewing speeches before the big presentation—not just showing up and winging it with some hastily scrawled notes. Like athletes taking numerous practice repetitions before they step foot on the field, Savage Leaders also prepare to ensure they are ready for when it counts. Savage Leaders also use mantras and positive self-talk to ensure they have the confidence needed to succeed.

In this chapter, we're digging into how you can prepare, practice, and perfect your mental and physical reps so you're ready to perform at the highest level possible.

USE AFFIRMATIONS TO BOOST YOUR CONFIDENCE

In 2017, Boston Celtics rookie guard, Jaylen Brown faced the daunting task of guarding basketball great, LeBron James during the NBA playoffs. According to an article on SportTechie, Jaylen had struggled with a fear of failure as far back as his high school days in Georgia and during his "one and done" year at Cal. "In high school, if I had a bad game, I couldn't eat," Jaylen told SportTechie. "It would be that bad with me. I wouldn't feel comfortable to eat because I felt that I didn't deserve to."

Through the help of mental skills coach, Graham Betchart, Jaylen turned to new methods to beat down the crippling fear. These methods have played a critical role in helping Jaylen tamp down the fear of failure and remain in a confident, ready state required to unleash his immense talent.

To mentally prepare for his tallest task to date—playing against one of the best players of all time in the playoffs—Jaylen needed something new and different to shift him into a higher performance gear. So Jaylen put a modern and Savage twist on using positive self-talk to boost his confidence, block out the fear, and get laser focused on facing LeBron.

He wrote and recorded a rap song called, "Building Blocks," where he raps about the importance of focus and breathing and keeping it all together. To beat back fear and get into the right state of mind, Jaylen would listen to his song on his headphones before each playoff game. While LeBron's Cavaliers ultimately prevailed and advanced to face the Golden State Warriors in the

2017 NBA Finals, the song helped Jaylen overcome his fear of failure and deliver a clutch performance.

Key Takeaway

Affirmations and positive self-talk increase self-confidence and your chances of success. Affirmations can take many forms, from a morning mantra to reading a powerful quote to listening to a motivational song. Employ them in a form that amps you up and gives you the mental edge that you need to dominate.

Savage Leaders use affirmations and positive self-talk to build and maintain confidence over the long haul, and to support their success when tackling new and scary challenges.

STRIKE A POWER POSE TO BOOST CONFIDENCE

Harvard researcher, Amy Cuddy introduced the "Power Pose" during her 2012 TED Talk. A Power Pose is a postural movement where you expand your limbs and spine as much as possible, standing with your feet firmly on the ground, shoulders thrown back, and extending your arms up and outward.

According to Cuddy, striking a Power Pose makes you feel more powerful. A feeling of power—which boosts confidence—will improve your performance. Since her TED Talk, leaders have created their own Power Poses that they use before going into a high-stakes situation. Several of my clients have also started employing simple Power Poses before high-stakes, and often scary, meetings. This one posture has boosted their confidence and performance.

Every edge counts.

Key Takeaway

Keynote speakers, top-notch negotiators, entrepreneurs, and business leaders use Power Poses to pause, feel big, and mentally prepare for a high-stakes situation or opportunity. Use a Power

Pose before a key meeting or event to boost your confidence and support your chances for success.

Savage Leaders use Power Poses to build confidence and thrive in key moments.

SIMULATE THE STRESS AND NERVES TO THRIVE WHEN IT MATTERS

For athletes, sporting events and most competitive endeavors trigger an avalanche of stress and nerves. That makes sense given the pressure to perform and win. To get ready, athletes prepare for months and years developing and honing their physical skills but also their mental capabilities that help them compete in front of thousands of screaming fans and live TV audiences.

San Diego-based therapist and women's volleyball coach, Dana Upton helps her team learn to deal with the intense pressure of championship matches by using practice time to simulate the stress and nerves her players will experience. "I have my girls run sprints and then get back into position to receive a key serve," she explained to me. "The sprint creates an elevated heart rate and blood pressure that is common to our physiological response to pressure and stress."

First, replicating the stress response enables her team to gain practice reps in the physiological state they will face during competition. Receiving a serve in practice without pressure fails to adequately prepare players for the actual game. Adding in the simulated stress offers her athletes a chance to practice in a fail-safe environment and readies them to perform in the clutch.

Introducing the physical symptoms associated with stress also enables her team to experience game-day pressure so that it feels familiar when they face it for real.

Key Takeaway

In business, you will face stressful situations that rattle your nerves just like an athlete. Pressure moments and times when we're asked to perform to our highest levels possible, strike all Savage Leaders.

You can—and should—practice and prepare for these pivotal experiences whether that's an upcoming presentation to your leadership team, a make-or-break customer meeting, or providing developmental feedback to a colleague. Simulate the physiological response to stress (elevated heart rate, heavier breathing, increased sweating) by briskly walking up a flight of stairs or doing 20 jumping jacks before practicing that moment. Yes, practice it by role playing, acting it out, and thinking through how you will approach the situation.

Savage Leaders replicate the stress response to create a no-risk practice forum before it counts for real.

WARM UP WITH AN INCONSEQUENTIAL ACTION

When your career or team's championship aspirations are on the line, the right warm up can make the difference between winning and losing.

Basketball players are well known for having scripted routines for taking free throws. Former New Jersey Net star, Jason Kidd, would blow a kiss to honor his family before taking a shot. There are a few reasons for using the same routine. One, routines help players to focus and block out the screaming fans waving inflatable thunder sticks and cardboard cutouts. Two, it's superstition. Three, it's also an opportunity, especially if a player enters a game cold, for them to get their arms and legs moving in an inconsequential manner before it really matters.

Besides Kidd, some basketball players will get into the zone, preparing for this key, high-intensity pressure moment by dribbling the ball and spinning it backwards, or fist bumping their teammates.

Similarly, a world-class public speaker who I spoke to also uses warm-ups prior to going on stage. Before any big talk, he will greet audience members and engage them in idle conversations. Doing so helps soothe his nerves. It turns neutral attendees into friendly faces, which gives the speaker confidence as he moves across the stage during his keynote.

It also allows him to warm up his voice ensuring that his tone exhibits the level of energy, engagement, and confidence that have vaulted him to the top—he's known as one of the best business speakers on the circuit today. Practicing and warming up his voice in inconsequential conversations with attendees allows him to walk on stage and deliver when it matters most.

Key Takeaway

If you experience a twinge of butterflies prior to key situations, try warming up with an inconsequential action before the next one. Create your own routine. For instance, find a friendly colleague in the lead up to the meeting and practice your tone and style with them on an unrelated topic. You can apply this tactic before presenting a controversial strategy to investors, pitching customers on a new product, or any other interaction that generates stress.

Practicing your tone, voice cadence, posture, and hand gestures ensures you are warmed up and ready to go versus booting-up from a cold start.

Savage Leaders find and use an inconsequential action to warm up and get a rolling start in advance of stressful moments.

ANTICIPATE AND PRACTICE FOR ALL SITUATIONS THAT MAY OCCUR

Michael, the NBA player who you met in the last chapter, gets ready for game day by practicing all of the scenarios that could come up during a game. "Every time I work out, I don't just shoot or dribble from one side of the floor. I learn to shoot from the right corner, the left corner, the top of the key, the free throw line, the mid-range."

He reinforces this by doing it over and over. As he said, "I practice making and missing. I lay down the platform before the game so when it's game time, I am comfortable because I have done it so many times. Once you are comfortable with that and you do countless reps and countless hours, there is no way you can't have confidence or believe in yourself."

It's those physical and mental reps done during practice that prepares him to take on elite competition and be successful.

Key Takeaway

You too can anticipate potential situations that might come up in pressure-packed moments and prepare for them in advance. For instance, prior to a potentially controversial meeting, seek out naysayers and people who likely have different opinions from you. These people can be inside or outside of your organization. Then practice your pitch to them and respond to their on-the-fly rebuttals. Doing this will decrease the likelihood of getting stumped by a tough question when the meeting happens. More importantly, you will gain experience and confidence developing cogent responses within a stressful environment.

To level up, practice with a rapid heartbeat and sweaty palms (see the previous insight). This will allow you to gain comfort amid the stress, so that you can deliver at a high-level during meetings.

Savage Leaders anticipate potential stumbling blocks and put in the work to practice their responses to those pitfalls in advance.

THE CHALLENGE: PUT IT INTO ACTION

In the lead up to a critical meeting, put in the time to take mental and physical reps to simulate what success looks and feels like. This moment could be cold-calling that one prospect who can help you crush your sales quota or speaking in front of a hostile crowd of experts on a new topic.

Commit to and perform one of the tactics described in the stories above, but be sure to tailor it to your own Savage Leadership style. Meditate for the first time, strike a power pose, or find a way to warm-up for that big moment, so you can be at your best when it matters most.

TAKE ACTION TO MAINTAIN AND REGAIN FOCUS

"Successful people maintain a positive focus in life no matter what is going on around them."

Jack Canfield

Savage Leaders possess the ability to focus over long stretches. This is crucial. In business, we inevitably experience ups and downs, or large spans of time between key pivotal milestones. Focus is needed between funding rounds, product design phases, and over short- or long-term projects with tight deadlines and seemingly never-ending daily distractions.

Accomplishing anything significant requires intense focus and the ability to avoid the deluge of distractions that come at us, digitally and from the people around us.

Staying focused is the difference between accomplishing big goals and being mediocre. It sounds simple, but focus requires intentional effort to stay on track and get back on it when obstacles get in our way. I'm talking external ones like difficult or demanding colleagues, competitors, and clients and even the internal ones like negative thoughts that we create and let creep into our minds. Focus also is key to avoid succumbing to the easier or more secure path as well as steering clear of new, enticing opportunities that can cause us to veer off course.

Staying focused is easier when we have the right tools and mindsets.

JOURNAL TO PRESET YOUR MIND

Golf is unique among major sports in that it requires steadfast focus for hours on end. Intense concentration for 60 and 70 shots over four hours requires not just focus during one shot, but also between them. Even hot streaks, which typically happen in short bursts in other sports, take place over an extended period of time during a round of golf.

As Duke Men's Golf Coach, Jamie Green explained to me, "One of our alums, Kevin Streelman birdied the last seven holes to win a PGA Tour event and it's still a record. That sounds so fast, but that had to be over an hour and 45 minutes."

That's one shot every three or four minutes. Compare that to other non-stop sports that lend themselves to constant focus throughout a competition. Golf has a staccato-like rhythm of shot, wait, shot, wait, shot, wait over the course of hours and days.

In my conversation with Coach Green, he explained the foundational work he does with his players on the mental side of the game to help them focus throughout a round and over a multi-day tournament.

Before Coach Green's players even step on the course, each of them dedicates time to ensure they are mentally prepared to excel.

Journaling is step one of the process and Coach Green requests each of them to "sit and put pen and pencil to paper" in order to start focusing their minds. As Coach Green says, "It [journaling] goes much further than people give it credit. When guys are willing to journal and focus on what they do best, and then focus on those things, bad things happen less often."

If you're a golfer, it's the bad shot that becomes a bad hole that can spiral into a disastrous round. Avoiding those "bad things" is critical to sustained success in golf.

Key Takeaway

Journaling has proven to be successful across all walks of life. Luminaries such as Albert Einstein, Marie Curie, and Mark Twain are well known to have kept daily journals. Science shows that writing by hand stimulates a part of our brains called the Reticular Activating System (RAS). Activating your RAS has shown to increase your focus.

Modern business leaders use frequent journaling to prepare for the day and to ensure they have the right mindsets for success. You can use journaling to focus your mind before a heavy day of strategic thinking or to adopt a competitive mindset required for a jam-packed schedule of sales conversations, tough negotiations, or where persuasion is needed.

Journaling can take many forms like stream of consciousness writing where you jot whatever thoughts and feelings come to mind first thing in the morning, in the evening, or before or after a big moment; reflections and expressions of gratitude for the day that just ended; or a focused and intentional effort to map out strategies and tactics to help you achieve your goals. You can journal in the morning or at night, during the day, and multiple times too. Use it whenever you need it.

Savage Leaders carve out time to journal as a way to gain focus on the day ahead as well as to reflect and learn from the past and apply it moving forward.

MEDITATE TO SLOW THE MIND AND FOCUS

Coach Green also advocates that his players meditate in advance of tournaments, before each round, and even between holes to maintain focus. Meditation helps his players remain centered or to regain it if it slips away. "It's trendy now to meditate and breathe, but there is no better platform [than golf] to see if it works as it takes four hours to hit a few shots," he said. "The guys that really dive into it see the fruits of it."

Coach Green's players have had great success using meditation to regain focus after a bad hole, a common occurrence for even the best golfers. The ability to bounce back from failure separates the top players from the pack. For Coach Green, bouncing back requires the same mindsets and techniques players used to prep for a round or tournament. "On the course, there are going to be opportunities to reflect on what happened," he explained. "What's their walking pace, breathing pace, and the song playing in their head and go back to those. They need to go back to what they can control and what they start with is their breath. If it's a bad hole, that is just a label and a feeling. It's going back to the breath."

"For a golfer, they can re-center and do some meditation on the course to get into that focused state," he continued.

The casual golf spectator only sees what's on the surface and misses all that goes on internally. "What we see from the outside is the energetic part, the emotion," said Coach Green. "We don't give enough credit to what players choose to think or say to themselves. Many times, a player curbed a meltdown that would have led him in the wrong direction. It [the meltdown] is almost always because things are happening too fast. Between shots and when a competitor is hitting their shot is when a player should be focused on slowing things down in their mind. That said, their pre-shot routine and the time it takes them to hit a shot should be the same or as close as possible to what it is when they play their best golf. Not faster or slower."

Meditation helps Coach Green's players slow down and regain focus so they can power through the full round of golf. It's that sustained focus players need to hit great shots, which lead to great holes, which lead to successful rounds, which end in tournament wins.

Key Takeaway

As a Savage Leader, you can use meditation in the morning to gain better focus on your key goals for the day. This will also reinforce the behaviors—like patience, active listening, empathy—that you want to practice with your teams, colleagues, and friends. Meditation also can help you regain focus if you get knocked off kilter after a lost deal, conflict with a colleague, or even a distraction in the office.

If you're not meditating, try incorporating it first thing in the morning for five to ten minutes, or right before a key task, or after getting off track. If you already use this tool, try it in a different context. For example, if you meditate in the morning to get focused on the day, try adding meditation before stressful meetings and events. Pay attention to how your focus and performance changes.

Be sure to block out time for meditating on your calendar to avoid getting swept up in the tasks and meetings of the moment.

Savage Leaders understand that stillness is a weapon that can focus their minds and negate the impact of negative thoughts and stress.

INDIVIDUALIZE YOUR APPROACH TO HELP STAY FOCUSED

One-size fits all approaches to leadership development inspired by the industrial revolution are fast becoming a relic of the past. Maintaining focus is no different, as it requires an individualized perspective for sustained success.

As Coach Green said, "It's not that players need to think one certain way in order to be successful. It's finding out and sticking to what players think and say to themselves when they play their best. So, it's more about being true to their personalities. Some players like to talk with their playing partners and if their playing partners don't care to do that, then we as coaches might stick around and keep them company," said coach Green.

On the other hand, "If a guy likes to be serene and calm in between and is playing with guys who are talkers, we (the coaches) might stay nearby to give our players a little buffer and to help them stay in their own space to remain calm."

For Coach Green, encouraging personalized routines for his players, based on their individual styles and preferences, is key to helping his players and the team maintain their focus.

Key Takeaway

As leaders, we each have our own needs and preferences when it comes to how we stay focused. You can apply this tip to your own life by flexing work habits to your individual preferences. Schedule tasks requiring concentration such as writing, planning, or strategic thinking when your focus is highest—in the morning, after an intense workout, or once the kids have gone to bed.

Also, seek out the atmosphere that is most conducive for you to focus. For some, it's sitting on a beach or at a local park. For others, it's as simple as firing up a Spotify or Apple Music playlist and listening to music on headphones while working in their home office.

Savage Leaders design their days and weeks to stay focused based on their individual needs and styles.

HIT RESET BUTTON TO GET BACK ON TRACK

Golf is a sport built on momentum. A bad streak can determine the outcome. "When things are going downhill, it goes fast," noted Coach Green.

Bad holes and streaks are a given, but players have to stop and turn them around before all is lost. That's why Coach Green arms his players with a series of mindsets and tips. It starts with each golfer having a plan for what they'll do when things go south.

The first step is a willingness to hit reset in the heat of competition. "You need to hit cancel and clear," Coach Green told me. "Hitting reset requires players to let go of what has happened that day or in the tournament thus far and to only look forward to what's next."

Now, that's easier said than done. Resetting the mind creates a void that needs to be filled with something positive. Coach Green encourages his players to fill the space with breathing and stretching—that helps them to let go even more of the past, focusing on the present, and preparing them for what comes next. Using stretching and breathing is key for players to re-center and recognize what they need to do when they are playing their best.

Coach Green also teaches his players to slow down—slow their movements, thinking, and emotions. "You don't see people in our game moving fast. When you go to a tour event, I am interested in how slow moving they are; moving from the practice green to the tee."

PGA golfer, Trevor Murphy, who played for Coach Green during college and who was featured in a previous chapter, puts this tip into practice during a round. "When you get under pressure, everything speeds up," he said. "When I struggle, I want to play faster, so I will walk slower, talk slower, warm up slower."

By slowing down, Trevor and the other players on Coach Green's team can hit the reset button, stopping the negative momentum.

Key Takeaway

Golf like life and business is full of moments that threaten to derail us. Losing your composure in front of your leadership team. Letting impatience over a customer's objections lead to visible frustration. Getting impatient with a teammate.

Savage Leaders acknowledge and accept this truth while creating a plan for when things go south. That plan is slowing down, stepping out of the situation, and regaining the center. If there is no room to create physical space and separation, then pause and take a breath. Breathe and focus on what you want out of the situation or the relationship.

Savage Leaders take action before situations spiral out of control. They slow down, pause, create space, and take a breath to refocus on the task or conversation at hand.

FOCUS ON WHAT YOU CAN CONTROL

In life and business, there is a finite set of things that we can control. Savage Leaders must learn to cede control over the things—people, situations, outcomes—that they can't do anything about.

As Coach Green told me, he teaches his players to recognize what they do have control over and to say, "I own these things." As he explained, "we want our players to be keenly aware of what they can control and what they cannot. You own and take charge of the things you can control, and you recognize that what is out of your control shouldn't deserve too much of your attention." Green went on to say, "You can't play defense and there is nothing you can do about the other players, the weather, the course conditions, or the course setup. We try to make sure our players feel empowered as much as possible and hopefully, reduce the time they feel like victims—or feel sorry for themselves—to very little or never."

Success in golf requires a steadfast focus on maximizing individual performance by knowing and owning what players have control over and not worrying about the other golfers and how they're playing.

Key Takeaway

As Savage Leaders, it's imperative to focus on what you can control and let go of what you can't. That's incredibly challenging, but focusing on things you can't control only creates stress and wastes brainpower. This applies in your day-to-day interpersonal actions as well as in how you approach professional development.

Let go of what colleagues are doing to gun for your job or what competitors are doing in the marketplace to insert themselves in front of your customers. Instead, focus on what you can do to get and stay ahead, and how your company can continue to out innovate the competition.

Savage Leaders commit time to tasks and factors they can control and let go of the rest.

THE CHALLENGE: PUT IT INTO ACTION

Commit to greater focus by applying one or more of the tips in this chapter. Consider the following:

- **Journal.** Schedule 30 minutes (or even 15 minutes) of journaling each day to plan the day ahead, reflect on what occurred yesterday, or to focus on the most critical task(s) that needs accomplishing that day.

- **Meditate.** Download a meditation app like Calm or Headspace and commit to 10 minutes of meditation to cap off particularly stressful days, or during lunch to re-center yourself for the rest of the day, or first thing in the morning to kick start the day.

- **Create an individual plan to put in action for when a situation spirals out of control.** Be sure to review it in advance of a particularly tense interaction with a prickly colleague or tough customer. After the fact, reflect on how it went and adjust the plan accordingly to ensure it supports your ability to stay focused and grounded when chaos surrounds you.

- **Write a list of items that you can't control.** For example, external marketplace factors, the outcome of a focus group with customers, how your colleague perceives your success. Also, make a list of what you can control like your attitude, how you show up with your teammates, what time you wake up, how hard you work. Commit to letting go of the things you can't control and focus more on what you can. For those items you can control, add corresponding tasks to your to-do list and block time off on your calendar to work on them.

DIG DEEP TO PERSEVERE IN DARK TIMES

"Many of life's failures are people who did not realize how close they were to success when they gave up."

Thomas Edison

Tales of start-up CEOs working ridiculous hours for long stretches of time are woven into Silicon Valley lore. We hear the stories of harrowing years-long sprints to find funding so companies could survive and then scale. We read about the many pivots in business models and go-to-market strategies that successful startups have endured. Innovators and inventors of all types are well known for their ability to persevere up, over, around, and through the unexpected obstacles and hurdles that stand between them and their visions for success.

Take Airbnb. Its founders endured humble beginnings and pivots that required perseverance while on the path to becoming the company it is today. Initially known as Air Bed and Breakfast, the company started as a way for its founders to help pay their rent by renting out air mattresses in their apartment during a design conference in San Francisco. After some initial interest, the founders set about creating a real company. It was slow to take off. To help stay afloat, they even repackaged cereal and sold it as "Obama O's" and "Cap'n McCains" during the 2008 Democratic Convention.

Eventually, one venture capitalist took notice of their unique business model and the founders were invited to Y Combinator, a Silicon Valley-based start-up accelerator. In the next few years, the company grew rapidly and was rebranded as Airbnb. Today the company is worth over 100 billion (As of December, 2020) and recently went public. To outsiders, Airbnb was an overnight success, but in reality, it required perseverance by the founding team.

Thomas Edison, one of the most famous American inventors, also provides a great example of perseverance. While he is remembered for his groundbreaking innovations such as the light bulb and alkaline battery, it was his ability to persevere that underscored his long-term success. Edison *failed 1,000 times* before successfully creating the first light bulb. In response to a question about his many failures, Edison famously responded, "I have not failed 10,000 times—I've successfully found 10,000 ways that will not work."

These tales of perseverance aren't just limited to innovators, entrepreneurs and startups. We've all heard about community and civil rights movements, led by men and women who tirelessly drive for change.

Despite the spotlight on world-changing entrepreneurs and these one-of-a-kind leaders, the ability to persevere challenges many of us. Most people give up when they face an unmovable business challenge, difficult work situation, or a ruthless and unappreciative boss. "It's impossible" or, "It just can't be done" or, "It will take too long" are common phrases muttered by people who can't endure the struggle and give up before seeing their goals through like starting a company, launching a new product, or landing a dream job.

But "when the going gets tough, the tough get going," as my grandpa told me when I was a kid, while he channeled his best Joe Kennedy (President John F. Kennedy's father and the person the quote is attributed to) impression.

Savage Leaders have an ability to persevere, endure the tough times, and get through to the other side.

PREPARE FOR THE DARK TIMES

Marathoners, triathletes, and other endurance athletes offer us a unique window into the powerful habits and traits that Savage Leaders can use to help get them through the dark times. To survive these grueling sports, athletes must persevere through intense daily training sessions and eventually the races.

I live in San Diego, a mecca for endurance athletes. I've enjoyed a front-row seat for the daily training of professional triathletes and the weekend warriors working to go faster and further.

Trevor Glavin, a retired XTERRA triathlete, got his start in triathlons after seeing a flyer about an upcoming event while studying at Cal Poly on California's Central Coast. He played sports growing up, but triathlons were a new challenge. "I was athletic as a kid, but I didn't know how to swim," he told me while discussing one of the many gaps he had to overcome before he could achieve success as a triathlete.

"I wouldn't drown, but I couldn't do much more than that," he said. "I got to know some Olympians at the time and I just fell in love with it."

Despite Trevor's lack of swimming experience, he worked hard to learn and improve. It paid off. He won a world amateur title in his first year competing. Eventually, Trevor turned pro and went onto become one of the premier XTERRA triathletes, landing in the top five overall in the U.S. series.

Being a professional XTERRA triathlete takes extraordinary work, strength, stamina, endurance, and focus. XTERRA events consist of a one-mile swim, a 20-mile mountain bike ride, and they conclude with a technical 10K trail run. Trevor didn't just compete; he was one of the best. I wanted to know what enabled him to reach the top of such a demanding sport.

He paused, reflecting on the question and his career. He kept coming back to one question. "Why did I have the ability to endure but others couldn't?" Trevor mused. "Is it something in me? I know incredible athletes who could never suffer through. You go to some pretty dark places during a race."

It was Trevor's ability to suffer through the dark places that helped him rise to the top. These dark places were triggered by the immense physical pain and extreme fatigue caused by pushing the human body to its limits. This led to intense psychological torment and thoughts that drove many of Trevor's competitors to quit and drop out during a race.

But not Trevor. He could suffer through the dark places because he had prepared for them.

Every night before going to bed, he visualized what it would be like in those tough stretches throughout the race. Trevor would envision the burning he would feel in his legs and lungs, and how he'd reach the end of his mental threshold for pain. As part of these "mental reps," Trevor would imagine the suffering that he would experience and the mindset he would need to adopt to prevail.

When race day came and the inevitable darkness arrived, Trevor returned to his nightly mental practice sessions, using them to pull him through. By experiencing that pain and suffering multiple times in his head, Trevor could resort to mental and physical muscle memory to support him during race time. "Doing the mental reps every night, I knew how to handle it [the dark times] and cope with it," he told me.

"I knew it would end at some point and I would just have to hang in there and get through it. There is always a lull when you can catch your breath and it will get easier like the downhill. I just had to hang in there."

Key Takeaway

As a Savage Leader, you may not be required to face physical pain and the mental torment like Trevor, but you will experience regular obstacles that require perseverance. You'll hear no after no, when cold calling new prospects. You'll read scathing reviews online. You'll receive negative feedback from bosses and peers. Preparing for those difficult and even scary moments is critical. If you don't, then those moments could derail progress and block your path to success.

Imagine a possible situation and all of the vivid details. What will it look like and how will you feel when it happens? Will you be nervous or scared? What negative things might people do or say?

Processing the situation in advance enables you to find peace and calm, if and when, those uncomfortable situations arise. You will have already experienced them, and you'll know what to do. Ultimately, preparing will allow you to be successful when it counts and persevere in the face of immense challenges.

Savage Leaders use visualization to prepare for dark times and to smooth out the path to success.

FOCUS ON THE PROCESS NOT JUST THE OUTCOMES TO MAINTAIN MOTIVATION

As a society, we are obsessed with external rewards, recognition, and achievement. We also hear competing advice to "enjoy the journey" or, "take a moment to smell the roses." Balancing the impetus for continued achievement while enjoying the journey is a real challenge for me, and for many of the leaders I've worked with.

One method to bring the two goals together is to focus on the process, not just the outcomes.

As leaders, hitting revenue and profit targets is key to company viability as well as job security. However, focusing on and rewarding the process is quite useful, especially when venturing into new areas that require us to stretch and grow.

Focusing on the process means we acknowledge the successes we have every day, giving ourselves a mental pat on the back.

This boosts our motivation to keep going and to persevere tomorrow and the next day and the next.

When I first started blogging, I was obsessed (like most people) with the number of views, likes, shares, and other outcomes. They felt personally and professionally validating. But when those numbers failed to measure up to my expectations, my enthusiasm for writing waned.

Fortunately, a friend and mentor encouraged me to celebrate the fact that I was pushing myself and putting content into the world. That was success in and of itself. Focusing on the process of writing and publishing each blog gave me the boost to keep writing. Along the way, the other metrics ticked up. Focusing on the process has helped me to persevere and gave me an early push to write this book.

Key Takeaway

Too often, we measure success using binary metrics. A salesperson hitting their quota, an author getting a book deal, a job seeker landing a job, an entrepreneur raising the next round of funding. These are great goals and there is no harm striving for them.

But if you solely focus on these metrics, they can drain you of your energy, commitment, and resilience to persevere through challenging circumstances. There are many factors outside of your control that can, and will, limit your success—the form it takes, when it comes, and how you reach it.

You can support your ability to persevere through these times by focusing on and celebrating the process, not just the end result.

Acknowledge that you're cold calling your most important prospects and not just the gimme's at the bottom of your lead list. Celebrate that you're expanding your network and meeting with new and interesting people during the job search process. Highlight that you're now regularly in front of the venture capitalists, who cannot just fund your company, but who can make the connections critical to your long-term success.

The point is to lose the singular focus on the outcomes, and learn to balance them with a healthy acknowledgement and celebration of the process.

Savage Leaders balance a focus on outcomes with acknowledgement and celebration of the process.

SET PROXY METRICS TO GAUGE FORWARD PROGRESS

One of the great advances of the digital marketing revolution is the ability of marketers to measure the progress of customers moving down the sales and marketing funnel. For instance, eCommerce companies measure front-end metrics like impressions and clicks followed by website engagement stats that show if a customer is moving through the order process culminating in a successful sale.

Here the only metric that matters is orders, but it's the insight from the other proxy metrics (impressions and clicks) that enable marketers and their website optimization teams to tweak prices and messaging to impact the all-important metric—conversion of a site visitor into a customer.

But this takes time to achieve—time that many leaders feel they don't have.

A few years ago, I worked with Brian, an executive who felt frustrated by his inability to deliver developmental and supportive feedback to his team that yielded positive results immediately. His goal was to be a great coach, and he used immediate results as the metric to gauge his ability. There was just one problem: his team wasn't achieving instant success. Brian quickly became mired in negative thoughts, believing his team wasn't developing fast enough.

I suggested that Brian step back and instead of using his team's immediate results as the litmus to how well he coached, that he set and create a proxy metric for his developmental efforts—similar to what eCommerce companies use. Brian decided to focus on and acknowledge the number of coaching conversations he held with his team instead of just the outcome of each meeting.

This seemingly simple shift stopped Brian from fixating on the end result. He still knew where he wanted his team to go, but he started seeing the smaller steps his team had to take on the road to success. As he focused on coaching his team through each important move forward, this boosted Brian's energy. He started to feel excited about working with his team, helping them to breakdown and find ways through obstacles, and to execute with more precision. It also took the pressure off each conversation, and Brian noticed that his team responded better to him, they listened and asked him more questions.

Slowly Brian grew as a coach. He learned how to be more present, to be a better listener, and to ask better questions that explored new opportunities with his team.

Ultimately, Brian became the coach he wanted to be by starting with an easier to achieve metric—a proxy metric.

Key Takeaway

You can apply the mindset of a digital marketer to your goals and aspirations by setting proxy metrics that indicate you're making progress toward your overall goals. For entrepreneurs in the process of raising money, a laser focus on the actual dollars raised can lead to a volatile cycle of extreme psychological highs and lows. Keeping an eye on proxy metrics such as the number of meetings with investors will help you persevere through what may seem like an endless and frustrating series of no's.

If you're in sales, try focusing on the number of meetings with connectors and influencers instead of a sole focus on deals won. Doing so will boost motivation while ensuring you are on the right path to achieve your goals.

Be sure that you select the right proxy metric(s) that correlates with the goal you're trying to achieve or will be evaluated on in your performance review.

Savage Leaders set proxy metrics to provide internal motivation along the path to achieving big wins.

FIND YOUR OWN REASON TO KEEP GOING

Movies like *Unbroken* (a movie about an American army officer who was captured during World War II and survives a series of hellish prisoner of war camps) inspire us with tales of extreme perseverance.

For each of us to prevail, however, we need more than a spark of inspiration. We need a personal reason to keep going when we're presented with easier alternatives and options to quit.

Even Navy SEALs, who get portrayed as superhuman on the big screen, need a reason to keep going during bouts of immense physical and mental fatigue. One Navy SEAL who I met, shared with me his unique reason to persevere during BUD/S training. BUD/S is a 24-week training and selection course that tests SEAL recruits' mental and physical fortitude. Only 25 percent of the recruits will pass. Those who do, endure extreme sleep deprivation, hours in the cold Pacific Ocean, and numerous activities that push them to their physical and mental limits.

"For me, it was thinking about filling out the paperwork if I dropped out," the Navy SEAL told me. "Quitting meant bureaucracy and for me that was far more painful than anything the recruiters could throw at me during Hell Week."

What motivates us to keep going during the difficult moments will vary from person to person. The trick is to find yours. It doesn't have to be a huge heroic reason either. Avoiding paperwork was not the over-arching reason for that Navy SEAL to stay in Hell Week. It was a micro-motivation that he drew on during the most intense moments. He laughed when he admitted that such a tedious task like filing paperwork was a ridiculous motivator, but for him, it worked.

Find your reasons to keep going and you can get through just about anything.

Key Takeaway

Everyone needs a personal reason to persevere when headwinds arise and momentum slows. We're all motivated and driven by different wants and needs. So tapping into our intrinsic desires can help us get through the more challenging times. For example, to achieve a promotion, you may have multiple motivations for putting in extra hours, working hard late at night and on the weekends. Maybe that promotion will allow you to move back to the East Coast, so you can be closer to your family. Maybe that promotion will provide the extra cash you and your spouse need to buy a new house. Maybe that promotion will enable you to take on a new role which is better aligned with your values and beliefs.

The *what* doesn't matter; just that it's personal and motivating for you.

Savage Leaders cultivate self-awareness and find those motivating reasons while aligning their goals with their values to persist over the long haul.

THE CHALLENGE: PUT IT INTO ACTION

The next time you find yourself wanting to give up out of frustration—like the challenge is too big, or you feel like you can't keep going—just *stop*.

Pause and reflect on what goal you're trying to achieve and why it's important to you. If it no longer aligns with your long-term plans and your purpose, consider scuttling it. However, if the goal is still worth achieving, take a step back and look for and celebrate the successes you've already enjoyed.

Also, set a proxy metric to provide a short-term boost and remove the "all or nothing" mindset toward achieving your goals. For example, set a goal to try a new communication style with a friend instead of with your boss at work. Or focus on new actions that you're taking like making cold calls, something you maybe had never done before. Celebrate the fact that you're doing it (whatever *it* may be). Tracking small wins can help you persevere in the face of challenging people, situations, and marketplace conditions.

EMBRACE AND UTILIZE PATIENCE AS A SECRET WEAPON

"All we need is a little patience."

Axl Rose

Patience.

Patience for change.

Patience for results.

It's an underappreciated attribute in a world that's constantly evolving, changing, and that demands agility, flexibility, and rapid responses.

Yet, the ability to be patient with your station in life, the progress your team is making toward developing a new product or service for your company, or the time it takes to gain a new skill is critical to your success as a Savage Leader.

When we lack patience, it can lead to poor decision making, undo pressure on teams, and internal frustration. All we see is the progress we haven't made in the timeframe we usually want. But greater patience leads to greater company performance through the development of better leaders and more engaged teams. Yes, we want a sense of urgency in a highly competitive and rapidly changing world, but we need to balance it with patience, especially when it comes to things out of our control—which is a lot more than we care to admit, and sometimes accept.

EMBRACE THE NOW

For Brian Smith, UGG founder, speaker, and author of *The Birth of a Brand*, patience can be found by embracing what he calls, "the tadpole theory." As leaders and as human beings, Brian says that we tend to dwell, and even obsess, on our future state, on what he calls "becoming the frog." But this future-focused way of living doesn't get us to our goals quickly. Instead, Brian writes in his book, "The quickest way for a tad pole to become a frog is to live every day happily as a tadpole."

That's a great line, but I wanted to know how we can be happy in our current state while staying true to ambitious goals. So I went to the source and asked Brian what he meant. "What I mean by this quote is to embrace the now, and learn from what surrounds you: the various universes coming into contact, the ideas being thrown around," he explained. "Don't expect it all to happen overnight. In the first years of entrepreneurship and starting a business venture, processes that will eventually become routine must be painstakingly developed by trial and error, and progress will seem to move at a crawl."

Brian's point is that we need to live in the moment and commit to being the best we can be every day as that tadpole. And eventually, we will become the frog.

Key Takeaway

Many people spend a colossal amount of their days fixated on becoming the "frog" and obsessing about their futures. Savage Leaders commit to being the best they can be in their current situation while constantly pushing toward their goal of becoming a frog.

Rather than obsessing about what you'll do when you arrive at your goal or becoming that frog, focus on what you can do now in your current career stage. For example, you might ask yourself,

"What can I do in my current role, or at my company, to deliver extraordinary service to our current customers now?" This focuses on the customers you have now, not just the potential ones that you want.

You can also ask, "What can I do in my current position to add exceptional value to my team and organization?" These questions start moving you down the path to becoming a frog.

Savage Leaders possess an unbridled passion for greatness, balanced with the patience to be comfortable with where they are. At the same time, Savage Leaders commit to being the best leaders they can be in every moment.

EMBRACE PATIENCE AS A TOOL FOR INDIVIDUAL EXCELLENCE

I used to say, "Patience is a virtue... for other people."

I embraced my impatience wearing it as if it were a badge of honor. It helped me to "get work done," I told myself and it helped me meet my need for achievement. At Accenture, it was also an asset to me, helping to drive projects to the finish line when we lacked resources, or when I had to manage last-minute client changes and other unexpected variables.

I used impatience as a constant prod to work faster and with greater intensity, to learn faster, and to pick up the pace in the pursuit of my goals and dreams. It was a tool that served me without question.

Or so I thought.

Over time, I started to learn that my impatience was undermining my ability to stay in the right state of mind when progress stalled or my goals flickered. This led to undue stress and an overwhelming sense of frustration in my current state.

My impatience also led to toxic thoughts like *why am I not there yet?* and *will I ever get there?* These thoughts didn't motivate me. They clouded my ability to be effective and productive, leading me to waste time—and sleep. I would lie awake in the middle of the night, thinking and worrying about things that were out of my control. Instead of acknowledging the progress I had already made and identifying what actions I could take to help move me toward my goals, my impatience paralyzed me.

I saw this so clearly in my work and career. I had spent years bouncing around and pursuing work which would inspire me and have meaning—but nothing seemed to fit and it felt like I would never reach my goal. Eventually, I uncovered my purpose or why—to help unleash the inner lion within leaders so that they can lead more authentic and joyful lives while creating stronger and more resilient teams, organizations, and communities.

Once I made this realization, it inspired me to shift my business from corporate consulting to executive coaching and training. I was excited, eager, and ready to live my purpose and meaning. But this didn't happen overnight—it was a process, a slow evolution more than a quick pivot. I wasn't prepared for that. It has taken me years to evolve the services I offer my clients. Sometimes, I've had to take on projects and clients just to cover expenses. This frustrated me. My days were still spent on clients and work that didn't allow me to fulfill my "why" and I grew impatient by how long it took me to change my business.

The source of my impatience was three-fold: part unbridled ambition and a steadfast focus on the end goal; part unrealistic time horizon to make the shift; and part unhappiness from being unable to serve clients in a more meaningful way (or so I believed).

One night, I realized that I needed to take on the tall task of practicing patience. As I did, I had an epiphany: there was a dichotomy between patience for action and patience for results. Impatience for taking action and not procrastinating is what helped fuel my early career successes and achievements. Impatience for results, which was often out of my immediate control, is what led to unproductive thoughts, emotions, and feelings that caused me to get in my own way.

Battling impatience has taken a great deal of effort. Applying many of the methods, mindsets, and tasks in this book has helped me battle back this inner demon.

So many of us (myself included) overestimate what we can achieve in one year and underestimate what we can accomplish in five years. This was the case for me and a near daily focus on greater patience has been helpful to keep a clear and productive mind.

For me, rather than zeroing in on the frustration of the slow shift to more meaningful work, I looked for opportunities to deliver the best service possible to new clients while still providing top-notch consulting to my full portfolio. Focusing on the reality of the business at the moment, rather than where I was going, helped instill a greater sense of patience while tamping down the frustration of not quite being "there."

It wasn't easy and it took regular reminders to focus on the here and now, but doing so has led to better results and continued growth toward where I want to be. It's taken years, but I've reoriented my company from its original focus on consulting, strategy, and project management to helping executives and their teams develop greater self-awareness, build trust, improve communication, and establish accountability. I still have long-term goals and aspirations for my work, but I know and accept that those won't happen overnight. They will take time to develop and grow, and I do that by taking action every day in their direction and by practicing patience.

The more patience I have cultivated, the more it has helped to ease my mind and dial back the frustration that would so regularly intrude into my daily life—and sleep. More patience has led to greater productivity, improved execution, and ultimately, greater joy and happiness.

Key Takeaway

A lack of patience can undermine your success. It can lead to poor choices. You may also place undue pressure on yourself, causing greater stress and anxiety—which will stop you from being the best leader you can be.

Savage Leaders recognize patience as a virtue, but make a distinction between patience for action and patience for results. Savage Leaders are both thoughtful and action oriented, but they also accept that results may take time, especially when it comes to shifting behaviors, careers, and organizational cultures.

Without results, no one would be successful, but fostering greater patience will ensure you're even keeled and maintain the right mindset needed for success. Boost your individual pursuit of greatness by practicing patience in achieving challenging goals, but maintain a steadfast focus on taking action that will lead to the long-term achievement of your big goals.

Savage Leaders balance an impatience for action with patience for results to maintain a mindset that's productive and enables peak performance.

FOSTER GREATER PATIENCE WITH YOUR TEAMS

Savage Leaders don't just practice patience for themselves, they nurture it among their teams. Billy McKnight, current head coach at United States Basketball Academy and Former Prolific Prep basketball head coach, preaches patience as a key to peak performance. "We live in a microwave society where everyone wants it to happen right now," Coach McKnight told me during our conversation. "Patience is everything in our developmental process. It's important to note that patience is a two-way street. It must be displayed by both the coaches and the players."

Coach McKnight transformed Prolific Prep into one of the nation's top prep schools to incubate future college and NBA talent. In his role at Prolific Prep, Coach McKnight led his team of elite high school athletes through an arduous annual schedule of over 180 practices, daily strength and conditioning drills, tournaments across the U.S., and countless hours studying film. His mission was to help his players develop the skills and mindsets to land Division I college scholarships and eventually fulfill their dreams of playing in the NBA.

As Coach McKnight knows, improvement doesn't come overnight; it's achieved through sustained effort over time and with an ample supply of patience.

Most players come to Prolific Prep for their senior year to develop the skills and mentality needed to play in college and the pros. One year isn't much time to make key changes that are needed at the next level and beyond, and the additional pressure of the recruiting process makes patience difficult to practice. "Ninety percent of the kids who come into college are not ready to play college basketball mentally," Coach McKnight said.

"So much of players being offered a scholarship is based on evaluating their athleticism and projecting what that player can become. My goal is to teach them what they would learn in college ahead of time so they are ready to contribute on the floor the first day they step on their college campus," said McKnight.

Coach McKnight ensured his players were ready by helping them develop the proper mindsets and skills to make an immediate contribution to their college team and to be recognized as a future NBA player.

To prepare them, Coach McKnight and his staff spent countless hours providing real-time developmental feedback. As Coach McKnight explained, "If they take a bad shot, you stop it and correct it. That happens throughout the whole year. Maybe they are screwing it up 98 percent of the time when we get them, but hopefully they are only making mistakes two percent of the time by the end and they know they've made a mistake before we even have to tell them."

Getting players to buy-in to an approach focused on constant feedback and adjustments was key to instilling patience with the process. A major factor in being able to provide this feedback without his players tuning him out was the way in which Coach McKnight conveyed the message.

"Players take on the emotional state of a coach," he said. "If they see that I'm frustrated, then they will get frustrated themselves and give up on the process. Learning has to be a positive, not negative experience, and the more they know they are progressing, the hungrier they will be for more feedback."

As he explained, "Who would want to go to practice if they just get brow beaten every time that they step on the basketball court? When corrections are made, they have to be made in a calm, clear, and hopefully, positive way. The tone of my voice is of the upmost importance."

Coach McKnight explained his approach of giving feedback with an example. "If a player throws the ball out of bounds for a turnover I won't yell, 'Stop turning the ball over!' Instead I'll say, 'What did you see there? What were you reading from the defense to make that decision?' Sometimes the player may have actually been making the correct read but their execution of the pass was just poor fundamentally. This is the perfect time to tell them, 'Fantastic! You made the right read. Last week you wouldn't have seen that. Now just concentrate on making an accurate pass.'"

With one simple statement, Coach McKnight helps his players see and acknowledge noticeable progress while simultaneously providing direction to them so they can take the next step in their development.

"I actively seek out these opportunities to show them that they've made progress," he said. "In fact, many times when I stop practice, it is strictly for that reason…to point out something positive that the player did. I'll do this in front of the whole team so that the team knows that player is making progress as well. If the player has made a mistake earlier in practice that needed correction, the next time they're in that situation and do it correctly, I'll stop practice 100 percent of the time to point out the positive play they've just made. So now they are seeing progress daily."

Taking time to intentionally acknowledge progress helps instill greater patience in his team and gives them confidence they can continue growing.

According to Coach McKnight, the teaching process cannot happen if he's unable to be patient, show restraint, or attack the problem in an intellectual way. He also pointed out that screaming, being derogatory, or throwing tantrums can never happen. "If I, as the coach, lose my patience and frustration surfaces, it becomes a drag on being able to convey my message because my players' mentalities will become negative," he said.

With his players, Coach McKnight preaches patience and taking joy in getting better every day. "You better enjoy the developmental process as there is a ton of pressure out there for immediate success," he said. "Parents, social media, peer comparison, and the pressure that the players put on themselves are all distractions to the ultimate goal. A lack of patience leads down the path to frustration and a negative mindset that ultimately will cause them to give up. Patience is a necessity. It's not optional."

Though Coach McKnight practices patience with his players, there are some things he has little patience for: a lack of effort, a poor or selfish attitude, not being on time, stealing from a teammate, not being thankful, treating others poorly, and other attitude-related issues.

The patience practiced by Coach McKnight and his players resulted in 17 of his players landing full-scholarships at top-notch college programs including Duke, Kansas, Xavier, Ohio State, and Oregon. Coach McKnight's players including Josh Jackson and Gary Trent Jr. have also gone onto get drafted into the NBA after only one college season.

Key Takeaway

Leadership requires not just practicing patience for one's self but with everyone. Savage Leaders provide time and space for their teams to grow and develop and give specific developmental feedback along the way—and they do it by demonstrating patience like Coach McKnight.

Savage Leaders focus feedback on the individual steps someone can take to achieve an outcome, not just on the results. For example, Savage Leaders can provide feedback on the quality of a slide presentation that a team member developed for a customer pitch, not just feedback on the outcome of the pitch. Doing so has two key benefits: (1) it shows patience in the process toward achieving results; and (2) it provides detailed feedback on what can be improved to support a successful result the next time.

Savage Leaders understand that results don't appear overnight and practice patience both with themselves and their teams.

THE CHALLENGE: PUT IT INTO ACTION

Practicing patience is challenging, especially for those of us not known for our calm demeanor and easygoing approach to life. To improve your ability to practice patience, try one of the following:

- **If you feel stalled in your current role and are frustrated by the lack of progress toward your next promotion, ask yourself, "What can I do in my current role to go above and beyond what I have done in the past?"** When asking this question, release the judgment that you should already be in a better position or further along. Instead focus on what you can do here and now to excel. Commit to action and make a note in your calendar to ensure you're accountable to making a change.

- **If you feel frustrated by your progress toward a current goal, take a few minutes to journal.** In journaling, note what steps you have taken to achieve that goal and what successes you have had to date. Don't just focus on whether you've achieved the ultimate goal, but consider what steps you've already taken that needed to occur to push you forward. Be sure not to just document those successes but acknowledge the time and effort you put in to take those forward steps.

- **Praise and coach the next time one of your team members fails.** Whether they fell short in completing a task, gaining alignment around a new idea, or executing a responsibility, first take the time to acknowledge what they did well. Then move to coaching your teammate on aspects of the process or execution that they can improve for next time. This approach shows your patience in team member's pace of development while giving them specific steps they can take to improve their performance moving forward.

SAVAGE PRINCIPLE #9

SEEK OUT DISCOMFORT TO DRIVE GROWTH

"Growth and comfort don't co-exist. That's true for people, companies, nations."

Ginni Rommety

As we become established in our careers, our growth tends to stagnate. We settle into routines doing many of the same tasks, day after day and year after year. We also take fewer risks such as leading ambiguous, challenging projects or taking on elevated roles associated with a high degree of failure. We may do so out of fear of tarnishing our well-crafted reputations. We may have greater family responsibilities and growing financial commitments.

Compounding the personal growth plateau is often the lack of true coaching and training provided by companies. At best, most companies equip their employees for the jobs they have and the skills needed in the moment, not for what could be coming or the agility needed for an uncertain future.

Savage Leaders find ways to continue to grow, both to succeed in their current organizations and to ensure a continued upward career arc. Finding and embracing opportunities that create discomfort is a pathway to ongoing growth and development.

FIND COMFORT IN THE DISCOMFORT

Navy SEALs are famous for thriving in hostile, chaotic situations, where conditions change minute-to-minute. In reflecting back on his career, Thaddeus, a former Navy SEAL told me, "The one word I would use to describe my career as a SEAL is *'uncomfortable.'*"

"What do you mean?" I asked.

Throughout SEAL training there was constant discomfort, Thaddeus told me. Shivering and cold in the San Diego surf. Rolling around in the sand and getting covered head to toe with it—what SEALs dub a "Sugar Cookie." Carrying around heavy logs, suffering extreme fatigue, and sleep deprivation in an exercise called "Log PT."

To make things worse, the exercises constantly change to maximize the difficulty and push SEALs to their mental and physical limits. The notoriously hellish BUD/S training is designed to help SEAL team members develop a mindset of "comfort in the discomfort."

The constant pain and discomfort that SEALs experience during training isn't without its merit. It is intended to mirror the conditions SEAL teams will experience on deployments: less than ideal sleeping conditions, extreme temperatures, and the mental stress of war and constantly changing battlefield situations.

"People always ask me, 'How real are the movies?'" Thaddeus continued. "Some are pretty accurate, but they only show a short montage of the cool stuff that we do as SEALs. They don't show the five hours riding in a tiny boat being cold, soaked, and seasick that comes before doing the cool things."

The ability to handle unremitting change and discomfort also enables SEALs to learn new tasks in real-time in a pressure-filled environment. As a SEAL sniper, Thaddeus regularly had to learn how to work with new weapons and systems. To do so, he leaned on his ability to deal with change and discomfort. Being confident despite a bevy of new variables allowed him to take on new, challenging tasks that ultimately supported his success as well as that of his team.

Learning to manage through discomfort also supports good decision making amid "the fog of war," where there is never a clear picture of what the enemy is doing while the conditions on the ground rapidly change. Training for discomfort allows SEALs to confidently make decisions despite an imperfect view of the battlefield, enemy locations, and exit routes. In Iraq, Thaddeus was tasked with building tactical plans for a rapid response team, which factored in the uncertainty of enemy activity. Success required a level of comfort with less than perfect information and creating 80 percent of the solution where the remaining 20 percent would be figured out on the fly.

Having confidence amid the uncertainty allowed Thaddeus and his team to successfully lead missions while minimizing casualties for both American soldiers and Iraqi civilians.

Key Takeaway

Frequent exposure to new and uncomfortable situations fuels growth by allowing us to practice new behaviors and skills that build muscle memory and confidence. As Navy SEAL training demonstrates, regular discomfort also fosters a mindset of "comfort in the discomfort," which enables SEALs to be equipped for change and uncertainty, leading to learning and better decision-making when conditions are constantly shifting.

As a Savage Leader, you can also benefit by immersing yourself in dynamic environments that are constantly changing and that require you to gain comfort in the discomfort. You can train for discomfort by taking on projects outside of your role at work or by challenging yourself outside of your job. You can: sign-up to speak to new groups on topics outside of your sweet spot; write a book or blog on subjects unrelated to your job; take classes in computer science, anthropology, and epidemiology or other subjects outside your traditional zone; or take on new health and fitness challenges.

Stepping outside of your comfort zone will help you to create mental agility while becoming more comfortable in constantly changing environments. This will yield better performance during times of uncertainty and rapid change in a work context—you'll already have trained for change, so you'll know how to overcome and manage any fear, uncertainty, or unpredictability.

Savage Leaders seek out dynamic, rapidly changing environments to gain comfort with change and to develop the ability to adapt to an uncertain workplace and future.

JUST SAY YES

As I sat in the back of the conference center, my palms were sweating and my heart pounded as stress induced adrenaline surged through my body. I had spoken in front of large groups in the past, but this was the biggest audience with some of the most influential executives and leaders who I had spoken to. I was also covering a new topic.

I was definitely in a state of discomfort.

Why the f*ck do you do this to yourself, time and time again!? I thought as I mentally ran through my 30-minute talk. I started beating myself up for all the constant challenges that I often put myself through. I regularly step outside of my comfort zone, testing myself over and over again with tasks that require me to do something new for the first time. It's hard. In that moment, I regretted saying yes to speaking at this event. I was worried that I would bomb in front of a room full of limitless business potential.

To help restore my mindset to confident and assertive, and to calm my nerves, I walked outside of the hotel, where the event was taking place, and took a slow lap around the building. Revisiting breathing techniques that I learned from Navy SEALs, I slowed my heart rate and returned to a baseline state of readiness. I reminded myself that I had thoroughly prepared for this moment. I had spent hours researching and honing my remarks for this audience. I had practiced my speech in different environments, and I had asked for feedback on my content and delivery from mentors and peers.

I was ready for the moment, and walking back into the hotel, I told myself I was ready to go—but honestly, I was still nervous.

When it was my turn to take the stage, I walked to the front of the room, stared at the group of ready, yet tired-looking executives and began my presentation. My voice wobbled at first, at least that's how it sounded to my ears, but calm eventually took over. I focused on connecting with the audience and ensuring they walked away with a valuable lesson—how they could apply a coaching framework with their teams and company.

My 30-minute speech went by quickly, and before I realized it, I was thanking the conference organizers, packing my things, and sliding into the back seat of an Uber. Relief washed over me as I headed to the airport.

Back home, a packed calendar didn't give me time to reflect on what had happened. But over the next few weeks, I processed that moment as well as other similar ones. I came to realize that it is the challenging moments in our lives that allow us to grow the most. More precisely, it's those times and the associated *discomfort* that provide the catalytic fuel for growth and development.

We may want to avoid these moments, but it's those times when we're put on the spot to lead a project or do something outside of our comfort zones that we don't think we're quite ready for, that offer us the best opportunities to grow and develop. It's the unexpected promotion due to a boss's departure, or a new and bigger project or task that triggers fear and discomfort.

But instead of saying no to these opportunities, if we say yes, we position ourselves to improve and expand in ways we can't imagine. For me, I gained greater confidence that I can speak to large, high-level audiences, which can provide more business opportunities that were previously inaccessible. After that one speech, I started saying yes to other opportunities that were both exciting and uncomfortable. Saying yes, when my natural instinct is to say no because I haven't done it before, or it's outside of my expertise, or I just don't feel quite ready, has helped me to quiet the voices of doubt and access new growth opportunities.

Regularly experiencing discomfort allows me to continue learning and growing in ways that a course, book, or conversation with a mentor can't. It doesn't feel great in the moment, but I always emerge battle hardened with new skills and more confidence to take on increasingly tall tasks. Defaulting to saying yes when presented with new and scary opportunities forces me to stretch myself to develop new skills, acquire new knowledge, and expand my leadership abilities.

Key Takeaway

Discomfort is the catalyst for growth and development. It pushes the boundaries of what you think you can do and challenges your notions of what's possible in your career and life.

Discomfort creates growth and also ensures your success in the task by forcing you to step up your game through better preparation, more practice repetitions, the acquisition of new knowledge and insight, and through more intentional effort and focus.

Accelerate your growth by saying yes to new opportunities, especially those that create a sense of excitement and potential as well as fear and discomfort. Hedge any risk by putting in extra work to prepare for those opportunities. Speak to mentors, read books, and conduct extra research. That fear will drive you to double down on your efforts and prep to support your success and more importantly, help you grow along the way.

Savage Leaders say yes to new opportunities that are exciting, offer growth potential, and trigger discomfort.

DON'T BE AFRAID TO MAKE THE BOLD MOVE

For Amir Sarhangi, who sold his company Jibe Mobile to Google in 2015, operating in a place of discomfort has always been key to his growth and development. Amir moved to the U.S. from Iran in fourth grade and was immediately put into an English-speaking classroom filled with native English speakers. Learning the language and adapting to a new culture was uncomfortable and one of the earliest challenges in his life.

Amir would go on to thrive in college at Cal Poly and after with early stints at Deloitte Consulting and Vodafone. Eventually, he became enthralled with the potential of entrepreneurship. On a trip to Iran, Amir and his dad discussed starting a chocolate company given the dearth of tasty confections in the country. Tragically, Amir lost his dad in an accident shortly after his dad, mom, and sister moved back to Iran, and the father-son dream of creating a chocolate company never came to fruition.

But losing his dad ignited the entrepreneurial spark into a wildfire of ambition. After graduating college, Amir started his first company, with his uncle. They focused on disrupting the real estate market with new technology. Unfortunately, the venture never got off the ground. According to Amir, "I made every mistake possible. I jumped in way too fast and was too eager."

When he launched Jibe Mobile in 2005, Amir was better prepared. He'd already been through tough, challenging times— losing his father and one unsuccessful company. Amir was also used to pressure. Since his father had passed away, he had the additional responsibility of supporting his mom and sister. Being an immigrant, losing his father far too young, failing at his first start-up, supporting his family—all these experiences created a boulder-sized chip on Amir's shoulder that drove him forward and beyond the fear of failure or holding himself back.

Jibe Mobile became successful, partly because Amir consistently put himself in a place of discomfort by taking bold moves. "You have to put yourself in a place where you are not comfortable," he said. "It's easy to get into a groove where you know people well and can keep getting stuff done. If you are not uncomfortable, you are not getting 100 percent of what you have."

In 2011, he put this mindset (discomfort paired with boldness) to the test. At the time, the company was focused on building text messaging services for big mobile carriers like Vodafone and Verizon. As Amir said, "We thought we could only survive in the messaging app space as companies like Ericsson and Alcatel were already in the platform space and we thought it was impossible to compete."

But through ongoing conversations with carriers, Amir and his team saw that the carriers messaging platforms were built with archaic technology that could be improved. Armed with this insight, Amir thought the company should instead build a completely cloud-based platform, much like Salesforce did to disrupt the Customer Relationship Management space.

As he explained, moving to the cloud was a bold move, but Amir thought it would be tough for the big players to quickly mirror—the transition would be disruptive to their financial reporting. Additionally, the shift to a radically different revenue model would launch fierce resistance among sales staff who rely on the rewards of large commission checks.

Amir saw a window for Jibe Mobile, but to capitalize on it, he had to be comfortable in the discomfort to make the bold move.

He did both and the company thrived. Making the bold choice for Amir was easier for a few reasons. First, he surrounded himself with a team he could lean on and trust. In particular, it was about, "Being able to share the journey with co-founders with staying power," he shared. Having partners to lock arms with when facing uncertainty and discomfort helped motivate Amir and gave him the courage to keep going.

Second was his positive mindset. Amir noted the importance of focusing on the positive and downshifting focus on what could go wrong. "Startups have to be super focused on fine tuning their business model and strategy and they have to focus on the upside versus worrying about what could go wrong— because just about everything will go wrong."

Third, Amir spent time ensuring his team could also find comfort in the discomfort. As a leader, it was critical for him to give his team confidence that the path forward would be successful. "I constantly tried to paint a positive picture for the team, giving them hope for how I saw our path to success," he said. "The minute the team loses its ability to trust its CEO, and their confidence in the way they see the future—game over."

Ultimately, Jibe Mobile outmaneuvered the titans by pivoting and moving into a much bigger opportunity. Since the acquisition, Google has used the technology built by Amir and his team to bring next generation messaging services to Android (Android Messages is the default on all Android devices) and mobile carriers around the world. To date, Android Messages has been installed over 3 billion times.

Amir left Google in 2018, and is currently an advisor for early-stage startups in Silicon Valley such as Zya and Virtual Visions. He is also the Vice President of Product for Ripple, a Fintech company helping customers send money globally using the power of crypto and blockchain. Amir's new role has been a different challenge and being immersed in discomfort has helped him continue to grow. "The whole thing is discomfort," Amir said. "I moved to a completely new industry with an unproven technology in blockchain and crypto currency with the added complexity of limited regulatory clarity."

He has also taken on additional projects outside of his role to "keep the edge," as he told me, but as Amir noted, "Nothing can ever be as stressful as being the CEO of a startup." Amir continues to look for opportunities to push himself out of his comfort zone as a way to grow and get the most out of himself. Discomfort in life and in business is the catalyst for exponential growth and success.

Key Takeaway

Don't be afraid to make the bold move, the one with bigger challenges, just because it causes discomfort. Take an honest assessment of both the opportunity and the challenges presented by assessing every available option. Then don't fear the audacious choice. Embrace it!

Often, it has considerably more upside and the challenges aren't as perilous upon further inspection. Making the bold choice may be easier when you surround yourself with a great team, board of advisors, or at least a friend who will hold you accountable to your commitments while cheering you on along the way. Maintaining a positive mindset will also help as you take on this new, scary challenge.

Savage Leaders don't cower away from the bold choice. They say yes, and they rely on their teams for strength and support to help them maintain comfort in the discomfort.

THE CHALLENGE: PUT IT INTO ACTION

Growth and discomfort truly are mutually exclusive. Turbo charge your development by seeking out new opportunities to evolve through discomfort. When that next one comes up, say *yes* and commit! To ensure you're successful, put in extra work by conducting additional practice repetitions, talk to mentors and experts in the area, and do research around the topic. Commit, not to just taking these actions once, but make them a part of your life and career moving forward. Default to say yes, when you might otherwise say no out of fear.

SAVAGE PRINCIPLE #10
OWN AND CHALLENGE LIMITING BELIEFS

"If you hear a voice within you say 'You cannot paint,' then by all means paint, and that voice will be silenced."

Vincent Van Gogh

Savage Leaders desire to be great.

While many of us have that desire in spades, we often can get tripped up and mired in the tar pits of self-limiting beliefs and negative self-perceptions. Self-limiting beliefs can stem from an array of sources, usually starting in childhood. Seemingly innocent comments from teachers or parents such as, "Joe just isn't very good at math" or, "Our family isn't successful" or, "I just don't have luck on my side" can plant the seeds inside of you that grow into a gnarled brush of self-limiting beliefs and blockers that hold you back—some seeds become so deep rooted that they might prevent you from taking that first step toward change.

Self-limiting beliefs are the single largest impediment to growth and success and can ultimately choke off your ability to become a Savage Leader. Eliminating, or at least beating back, those thoughts and beliefs is critical to achieving your potential and reaching your definition of greatness.

ASK YOURSELF, "HOW MIGHT THAT WORK?"

According to serial entrepreneur, Michel Kripalani, self-limiting beliefs are a part of the human condition and often stem from childhood. "It starts all the way in childhood from everyone who is teaching us," he said. "Whether it's parents or teachers, we put them on a pedestal."

As kids, most of us believe that our parents can do no wrong and that they wear an "S" on their chests like Superman and the superheroes we idolized in our youth. As we grow up, we learn that our parents are, in fact, fallible yet we continue to elevate and idolize other people. Think movie stars, Silicon Valley titans, and leaders in our communities, who we may see as more successful than us. Anytime we put others above us, it threatens to hold us back. As Michel explained, "As we get older, there are always people that we look up to, whether it's people who have written books or more successful CEOs," he said. "It's common for me to think that I haven't done enough to justify standing on stage, or writing a book, or starting a company of that scale."

The more we look outside ourselves at everyone else, the more we believe that they have something we don't, and we doubt our capabilities to soar to the same great heights. Toxic thoughts such as "I'm not ready" or, "I don't have enough experience" or, "I'm not talented enough" can hold us back. We may stick to the status quo, aiming for smaller achievements rather than elevating our gaze and taking on bigger, more ambitious, and even scarier goals—the kind that can profoundly change our lives.

If we can overcome our self-limiting beliefs, then we can move closer to realizing our dreams. That has been one of Michel's secrets. His ability to overcome his inner critic led him to follow a big, audacious dream. In 2009, Michel launched Oceanhouse Media, a gaming and app development company based in Encinitas, California. During the early stages, he and his wife, Karen went into a local Barnes & Noble with a yellow legal pad to write down content ideas that might work in an app. As they considered different possibilities, Michel's wife posed an ambitious one to him.

"How about Dr. Seuss?" she asked.

"Normally, I would have shot down that idea," recalled Michel, but instead of succumbing to self-limiting beliefs and saying, "That won't work," instead Michel asked himself, "How might that work?"

"My mind would have never gone there as my own self-limiting belief was that we had just started this business and we were nowhere near that league," he told me. "After considering it for a few moments, I realized that I alone was responsible for playing small and instead asked myself if we were to do it, how might that work?"

Asking himself an open-ended, possibility-generating question as opposed to a binary, yes-or-no one like, "Will that work?" started Michel and Karen down a path that would change the trajectory of Oceanhouse Media. They began brainstorming how a Dr. Seuss-centric app could come to life. In a story that only makes sense looking back, Michel recalled how 15 years before, he had been asked to sit on the UC San Diego Library Advisory Board. He further remembered that one of the largest benefactors, and a fellow board member, was Audrey Geisel, the widow of Theodor Seuss Geisel—otherwise known as Dr. Seuss.

Michel dropped a note to the head librarian asking if he was willing to introduce Michel and Karen. "It was almost like I was asking, 'Would you be willing to change my life forever?'" he told me.

Much to Michel and Karen's astonishment, the librarian said yes, and soon the couple was connected to Susan Brandt, who ran Dr. Seuss Enterprises. Flash forward just a few months and the duo found themselves closing a deal for the Dr. Seuss app rights, which quickly catapulted their company forward.

To date, Michel's company has developed and published over 600 apps for mobile devices including over 50 based on the Dr. Seuss books. In addition, he founded his second company,

Extality, in 2017 to design and develop applications for augmented reality and virtual reality. Michel is currently the CEO for both companies.

None of this would have been possible had Michel allowed his limiting belief to take control. "Self-limiting beliefs are extremely dangerous and they can do a lot of damage," he said. "At the end of the day, we are a lot more capable than we give ourselves credit for. It's really a matter of getting going."

Even today, after all of Michel's success, he still has to remind himself that he's more capable than he sometimes believes. "I still find myself thinking that I'll be ready to go on stage or write a book as soon as I make that multi-million-dollar exit or build the next business," he noted. "It takes me awhile to realize that I have been doing this [succeeding] for a long time, and I have had more than enough success to be influencing a large number of people on this planet."

Key Takeaway

We all have self-limiting beliefs that can act as obstacles to achieving our goals. Challenging those beliefs is critical. Instead of listing all of the reasons why an idea, action, promotion, or other opportunity won't work, ask questions such as, "How might that work?" or, "How might that be possible?" or, "Who else has done something equally crazy when they weren't ready?" Questions like these shift your mind from what is impossible to proactive, problem solving that is filled with possibilities.

Savage Leaders lean into the negative voices and ask themselves how something can be done, instead of focusing on why something is impossible.

SET MENTAL ANCHORS TO RESET YOUR BELIEFS

As my career transitioned from consulting to executive coaching, I realized that the ability to write and share my ideas was critical to help me achieve my goals. Unfortunately, I had a self-limiting belief that I was a weak writer, unable to express my thoughts and ideas in compelling and insightful ways.

This belief stemmed from my failure to gain acceptance into AP English in high school and my relative struggles in college English. Upon further reflection, I realized that the challenge wasn't with writing but in my ability, or lack thereof, to analyze topics such as what Franz Khafka meant in *The Metamorphosis* (a story about a man who is suddenly transformed into a bug reflecting Khafka's feelings of isolation and inferiority).

My struggles in one area of my English courses cascaded to a negative self-perception about my ability to write and communicate successfully.

This belief acted as a mental anchor throughout my college years and into much of my adult life. It caused me to stay rooted in old models of what I could achieve and limited my potential. I knew that writing blogs and books would be key to helping me reach my goals, but the limiting belief was so deeply engrained that it held me back. These beliefs anchored me in the kiddie pool of what I considered mediocrity instead of diving headlong into the big, blue and often scary ocean filled with big challenges and big rewards. Writing and publishing content would expose me to criticism, but it also would provide an opportunity to create a name for myself and connect with clients and prospects in new ways.

The first crack in my self-limiting belief came through the support of my mentor, Annette. Early on, she identified "Communication" as a top strength of mine, stemming from the results of the CliftonStrengths Assessment, a personality assessment created by Gallup which identifies an individual's top strengths.

"Darren," she would say, "How can you use your communication talent to be successful with the task?" The more she prompted me to find ways to use this skill, the more I began tapping into my intrinsic ability to convey complex ideas and persuade people to action.

As a result of Annette's encouragement, I started believing that I possessed the talent to write and create. I started to study great writers of fiction as well as business and pop culture. The more I dug in, the more I realized a multitude of successful writing styles existed. Putting pen to paper is the ultimate creative endeavor that allows you to express your personal style and flair where there is no right or wrong answer–something we aren't taught in school!

Determined to leave my self-limiting belief behind, I wrote a blog for LinkedIn. I wasn't sure I wanted to post it. It was scary to share content to my highly-curated professional network. Concerned it wouldn't pass the "smart" filter, I worried that a poorly written article or misfire would ding my personal brand. I had spent years burnishing it with a laser focus on how each and every experience would look on my resume.

Luckily, a friend and colleague, David acted as my internal sounding board. He encouraged me to post it. To my surprise, it landed well with my network and others. That early win increased my confidence to keep writing and eventually the concern for whether or not I sounded "smart" subsided.

Writing a book would be a much larger endeavor. It would require me to commit to substantially more words (a blog post can run 800-1,800 words; a book north of 40,000). And I'd have to stare at a blank screen for extended periods of time. It was daunting, but I knew I had to go for it.

To help spur me on, I started slowly announcing my book project to friends and colleagues—my wife, family members, mentors, colleagues, and clients. Doing so forced me to not only commit to writing but also publishing the book. Inquiries about it and repeated questions like, "How's the book coming?" held me accountable and gave me the support I needed to keep going.

Making an ambitious commitment shocked my system and helped me slither out of the skin of my self-limiting beliefs.

No one is immune to self-limiting beliefs. Even the most successful leaders, entrepreneurs, entertainers, and athletes battle negative self-talk. Peel back the layers and you'll see that many successful people in our society today held similar beliefs, but proceeded nonetheless—and succeeded.

Key Takeaway

Self-limiting beliefs tend to emerge as we make difficult changes in our lives like accepting a new promotion, making a career change, or starting a company or a new project that will require us to develop and use different skillsets. You don't have to let the negative self-talk rule you. Challenge the "truths" by asking yourself questions like: "Is that really true or is that just someone's opinion?" or, "Does that really apply to me anymore?" or, "Is there any evidence to support that belief or is it all in my head?"

Also, force yourself to overcome those beliefs by making commitments that will allow you to challenge and rise above them—commitments to people you admire are especially powerful.

Savage Leaders look self-limiting beliefs in the face, don't accept them as truths, and make commitments to challenge and overcome them.

THE CHALLENGE: PUT IT INTO ACTION

Take a stand today and refuse to let self-limiting beliefs get between you and your goals. Take the first step by reflecting on any beliefs or doubts that you have about your abilities to achieve a specific goal, complete a task, or to make a big change. For example, thoughts such as, "I didn't go to a good enough college" or, "I'm not analytical enough" might hold you back from interviewing at your dream company. Other beliefs such as, "I don't have the track record or experience" might prevent you from starting your own company or throwing your hat in the ring for a big promotion.

Once you have identified one self-limiting belief, journal and reflect on the source of it and what data points (e.g. someone's opinion, a snarky remark made by a family member, or an old performance review) support that belief. You will likely find that the source of that belief isn't rooted in facts—it's probably based on someone's subjective opinion. (Warning: that opinion could be yours!)

Finally, make a firm commitment to take a specific action to disprove and overcome that belief. Share what you'll do with a trusted colleague or mentor so that they can cheer you on and act as a powerful accountability partner.

CRUSH YOUR DOUBTS AND REFRAME THEM FOR SUCCESS

"Doubt kills more dreams than failure ever will."

Suzy Kassem

All of us experience doubt. It's human nature for it to creep in from time to time, even the most confident elite athletes, serial entrepreneurs, corporate executives, and even military special forces face it.

Doubt is an unproductive emotion and cognitive state. The source of it is multi-dimensional, but one key driver is the self-limiting beliefs that we discussed in the previous chapter. If you leave them to fester unchecked, they can manifest as doubts across all aspects of your life and career.

Doubt prevents us from confidently vaulting into a situation, conversation, or taking on a new task or role with a mindset for success. Over time, it can lead to a crippling sense of fear that can stop forward progress.

Luckily, you can preempt doubt by addressing your self-limiting beliefs (see previous chapter) or by tackling them in real-time as they show up in your life through mindset shifts.

GET OUT OF YOUR OWN WAY

Former NFL star and TV personality, Michael Strahan has faced doubt throughout his life. Outside observers might scratch their heads as to how this charismatic, herculean man would ever face doubt. If you dig deeper, you will see that Strahan experienced challenges that sparked doubt along his path to success in professional sports and as a media celebrity.

Strahan was born in Houston, but spent many of his formative years in Germany as the son of an Army Major. Growing up, other kids teased him for being overweight. Eventually he grew tired of it and started transforming his body by watching Jane Fonda workout videos and clips of retired NFL running back Herschel Walker—a workout legend known for his daily regimen of 1,000 pushups and over 2,000 sit-ups.

A transformed physique allowed Strahan to tap into and unleash his natural athletic ability that had started to reveal itself at the tail end of his high school years. Strahan went onto play football for Texas Southern University and was drafted by the New York Giants in the second round. He earned the starting nod in his second year after notching just one sack during his rookie season. From there, Strahan's career ascended slowly, but his continued hard work helped him earn his first Pro Bowl appearance in his fifth season in the NFL.

Despite his success as an NFL player, Strahan experienced doubt about his ability to play at the highest level. To deal with it, he focused on positive self-talk. "It's about recognizing when you are doing those things to yourself and how to correct them and get back in line," he said in an interview on Big Think's YouTube channel.

After a great game against the San Francisco 49ers, Strahan said, "I felt horrible and didn't feel good about myself." After meeting with a sports psychologist, Strahan noted, "It reinforced that you have to speak kindly to yourself. Treat yourself and say to yourself what you would say to somebody else to encourage them. And that's what I started to do. The next week I had the best and greatest football game I had ever played. It was because I told myself 'you can do this, you know how to play this game, you belong in this game.'"

Strahan was selected to seven Pro Bowls during his career, set the single-season sack record in 2001, and eventually was voted into the Pro Football Hall of Fame. He overcame his doubt to have an undeniably successful NFL career.

After retiring from the NFL in 2008, Strahan pursued a career in media. He leaned on his playing experience and natural charisma to land his first role with FOX Sports as a football analyst. As he made this transition, doubt once again started to creep in. He wasn't sure if he could be a sports commentator. To help him overcome his doubts, Strahan returned to the lessons learned from his time in the NFL. That meant beating back his biggest enemy–himself.

"The biggest thing is getting out of the way of yourself," he said. "We limit ourselves more than anyone limits us."

Today Strahan is a successful media personality. In 2012, he joined Kelly Ripa on *Live! with Kelly* before moving to ABC's *Good Morning America* program. In addition to his co-hosting duties on the morning show, he also continues working as an analyst for *Fox NFL Sunday*, and hosts the television game show, *$100,000 Pyramid*. At every level, Strahan has faced and tackled his doubt. By doing so, he's overcome it and has gotten out of his own way. "I am as scared and fearful as anyone else to tackle something new," he said.

Yet persistence and the use of positive self-talk ensured Strahan could face down doubt and succeed at the highest levels of professional sports and television entertainment.

Key Takeaway

Doubt creeps into most of us. Doubt about our ability to grow a company, lead a team, take on a new role, or succeed with a different or challenging task. Those doubts may result from a lingering self-limiting belief or because we're trying to do something for the first time.

You can overcome them. It starts by pushing doubts aside and shifting from being your worst critic to your greatest cheerleader. Use positive self-talk to help you get out of your own way.

Savage Leaders recognize doubt as part of the growth process and find ways to squelch it by getting out of their own way.

RECAPTURE YOUR PAST, BEST SELF

Growing up, sports provided me with many powerful lessons for life and leadership. The best ones came from failures—not the wins and achievements, the raising of championship banners, or All-Star selections (although those were nice!). Rather, it was riding the bench my senior year in baseball after a childhood of successes, that drove home to me lessons of patience, persistence, and the criticality of hard work.

As the father of two athletic kids, I knew they would also experience the highs and lows of sports while learning important lessons about putting in hard work, being a good teammate, and sportsmanship. I also knew those struggles would help them grow. I just didn't know it would occur for a 7-year- old.

A few years back, my oldest son, Madden decided to try out for Encinitas Express, the local competitive soccer team near us in San Diego. After two angst filled days of tryouts, I received the call from Coach Jerome letting us know Madden had made the team! He was thrilled to be selected and to join several of his good friends on the team. The season started strong, but over the summer months, Madden's enthusiasm for the sport he once loved, dipped.

I started to also see some hesitation and doubt in Madden's ability to excel. Like adults, kids face doubts, even in something that adults think is trivial. Madden had been a top player and scorer in previous seasons, but something was getting in his way now. There were a number of possible reasons for his sudden confidence loss—playing with a team of alpha-athletic kids, the loss of one of his close friends and teammates to a broken thumb, or just maybe that Madden was only 7-years-old.

Regardless, as a father it pained me to see my son doubt himself and lose interest in his favorite activity. I didn't know what to do, so I pulled out his previous year's Blue Ninja jersey from deep in his closet and brought it to him. "Remember what it felt like to wear this?" I asked him. "Remember how confident you were and how well you played?"

He smiled as I could see him remembering the previous year. That brief look into my son's past helped him recapture himself and his confidence. It also brought back memories of fun and camaraderie and playing with his close buddies. Seeing his old jersey and remembering that experience seemed to reignite Madden's passion for the game too. He excelled the rest of the year and continues to love soccer—while learning lessons along the way. All it took to get him back on track was for him to briefly think about his previous successes.

Key Takeaway

All of us face doubts throughout life. Looking to the past for a situation or moment when you felt confident or had a win can help re-ground you. That brief reflection will also start chipping away at what blocks your momentum and progress now. That past moment could be as simple as looking at an old business card that reminds you of past successes or recalling a successful negotiation you had with a customer or supplier.

Savage Leaders use past successes, and more importantly, times when they brimmed with confidence to help push through challenging moments filled with doubt.

REFRAME DOUBT AS UNCERTAINTY

Doubt is toxic for entrepreneurs and business owners. It leads to inaction and decisions overly weighted by concern for the worst-case scenario. That's what happened to my client, Casey. He had recently launched a new IT services company focused on the

Northeast region of the United States. His goal was to minimize time away from his wife and their three daughters, and their lives in Connecticut.

Launching this company had created independence for Casey—a core value and a priority in his life at this time. He had grown tired of living out of a suitcase, being stuck in airports battling late-night flight delays, and doing whatever it took to move up the corporate ladder as a consultant at Deloitte Consulting. This new opportunity allowed Casey to utilize his consulting experience and the knowledge he had gained when he earned his MBA at the University of Michigan.

Casey has a magnetic personality and a healthy dose of self-confidence, but in getting to know him, I learned about the inner doubt he faced and how often it stood in his way. Casey spent countless late nights and early mornings with his mind flooded with thoughts about why his business wouldn't succeed, what could go wrong, and what people would think if he failed. Such damaging thoughts burned precious time, and crippled Casey's ability to take risks, make quick decisions, and tap into his vast skillset to grow his business—the vehicle that would enable him to create a well-balanced and meaningful life for him and his family.

Casey's company was well positioned to succeed given the explosive growth of clients adopting software such as Salesforce, Oracle, and SAP. Despite his strong track record and marketplace opportunity, Casey still doubted his ability to build his company. To address that doubt, Casey and I started to look at doubt from the perspective of probability. Doubt often stems from a less than a 100 percent chance of achieving a task or outcome.

In life and in business, nothing is truly a guaranteed success. We use the "slam dunk" analogy from basketball to indicate 100 percent certainty. Though basketball fans know that a "slam dunk" isn't guaranteed despite the athletic prowess of the player going for it. Likewise, despite the best plans or teams, the success of a new business or initiative launch isn't certain—it's uncertain due to internal factors as well as external ones such as macroeconomic headwinds and competitive actions.

Over the course of several conversations, Casey and I started teasing apart his doubts to separate those rooted in self-limiting beliefs, which needed to be addressed separately, and those that were truly due to uncertainty. For doubts based on uncertainty, such as the success of a new service or marketing campaign, Casey built contingency plans to make improvements on the fly to prevent failure.

Over time, he started to realize that many of his doubts were due to a lack of certainty and not a reflection on his skills and experience. This reduced his overall sense of doubt and provided a needed boost to his confidence.

Reframing doubt as uncertainty helped Casey overcome many of his own mental hurdles. As a result, doubt became less of a drag on Casey's actions and prompted him to make faster, more confident decisions. In the last few years, Casey's company has grown rapidly, gained marketplace recognition, and the path forward looks bright.

Key Takeaway

Doubt has the ability to get in our way and impede progress. It can feel overwhelming and frustrating, especially if it causes us to become indecisive or prevents us from taking action. Teasing apart our doubts and focusing on those rooted in uncertainty can reduce the mental stack that gets in our way. Uncertainty exists when there is less than a 100 percent chance of a project, initiative, or negotiation succeeding.

Start to address those uncertainty-based doubts by building plans to make the uncertainty more certain. You can conduct additional market research, get advice from mentors, and test ideas prior to a full commitment or roll-out in order to reduce the uncertainty.

Savage Leaders look at doubt through the lens of uncertainty to build contingency plans for dealing with and moving past the doubt.

THE CHALLENGE: PUT IT INTO ACTION

Take a stand and stop letting your doubts get in the way of achieving your goals. Start tackling your doubts by considering a project, task, or situation that prompts those feelings. Then, try one or more of the following:

- **As you think about the doubt that arises, use positive self-talk.** Say affirming statements like, "This may be the first time that I'm doing this, but I have taken on similar tasks in the past and succeeded" or, "I am good enough and deserve this upcoming promotion," or, "I have done all of the hard work, the preparation, and I am ready for this moment. It is my moment to shine!"

- **In considering the situation that sparks doubt, reflect back on past successes, and times when you had extreme confidence in a task or role.** Recall how it felt to be confident and powerful. Recapture that confidence by also considering the doubts you had prior to or in that situation. Keep in mind that most of us feel doubt before big moments, and that doubt is a part of anything worth doing. Be confident you'll succeed once again and make a commitment to take action, move forward, and overcome that doubt today.

- **If your doubt is due to uncertainty of an outcome, then consider what moves you can make to improve your chances of success.** Ask yourself, "Who has accomplished something similar that I can talk to?" or, "What information do I need to know to increase my odds of success?" or, "What is an assumption I might be overlooking that could be critical to my ability to succeed?" Use your answers to take action, increase the probability of success, reduce the uncertainty, and extinguish the doubt in your mind.

SAVAGE PRINCIPLE #12
MAKE FEAR YOUR FRIEND

"I cultivate it [fear], order it and use it."

Bobby Axelrod in the hit television series, *Billions*

Everyone experiences fear—left unchecked it can overwhelm us. Fear triggers physiological responses that range from sweaty palms to a pounding heartbeat and even the inability to move.

Fear strikes us at all ages. Even those of us lucky enough to grow up in stable households, get hit by fear in irrational ways as kids—nightmares about 10-foot tarantulas and maniacal carnival clowns. As adults, our fears evolve. We may fear physical harm, as we become more aware of our surroundings and about the realities of the world. Fear of embarrassment, failure, and shame may also take center stage.

In response to our fears, we can start changing our actions. Maybe we set more conservative goals, take fewer risks, say no to promotions or new responsibilities, avoid starting that company we've dreamed of, or refuse to change careers or take a job at a different organization. Ultimately, if we let fear reign, we can impede our progress toward personal excellence.

Savage Leaders tackle their fears, even using them to drive them closer to achieving goals and aspirations.

FIND SOMETHING FAMILIAR

As kids, we cling to familiar items to deal with the fear of the dark and other unknowns. My youngest son clutches a stuffed velvet eagle to help him fall asleep. The familiarity of his stuffed animal provides him with a sense of comfort.

As adults, we can also use familiarity to navigate through the hollows of fear. Thaddeus, a former Navy SEAL, learned in training to mentally latch onto something familiar to help pull him through new, uncertain challenges. When he faced a new assignment during BUD/S training, rather than be overwhelmed with the magnitude of the task, Thaddeus looked for an element of familiarity to generate the confidence he needed to keep going.

During one particularly brutal day, Thaddeus found himself sitting in the cold surf of the ocean and thinking, *Geez, I don't know if I am going to make it.* However, he knew that the next exercise was Log PT, where six to seven recruits would carry a 200-pound log for two hours while performing a variety of calisthenics.

Log PT was a known element to Thaddeus, and he was familiar with the exercise. Just knowing that helped make the unknown of what else was to come, less scary for Thaddeus. The fear of the unfamiliar often drives many aspiring Navy SEALs to quit. "Most people quit at the beginning of an evolution [during BUD/S training] as they build up the future pain to be worse than it actually is."

Thaddeus is describing the power of fear—how our thoughts can run away with us, creating outsized expectations about a future event that may not be true. The key to reining in our fears, Thaddeus told me, is to find familiarity or a familiar pattern. This will help to keep you moving forward through the fear.

Key Takeaway

We all face fear throughout our lives and our careers. Fear of a project failing. Fear of losing a deal with a new customer. Fear of pitching a deal to the biggest prospect to date. Embrace the fear by finding an element of familiarity. Ask yourself, "Is there some aspect of this project that I have previously completed successfully?" or, "Is there a similar deal I have closed in the past?" or, "Have I conducted a similarly challenging conversation before?" Finding familiar elements will help you proceed despite the fear.

Savage Leaders face their fears by looking for and embracing familiar elements to guide them forward.

SEGMENT THE TASK

Navy SEALs also help conquer their fear by breaking big, scary tasks or objectives into small, manageable chunks that aren't scary in isolation.

As Thaddeus recounted, segmenting is a key tactic SEALs employ to survive "Hell Week" during BUD/S training. SEAL coaches will direct recruits to focus on what is immediately in front of them to avoid the sense of overwhelm that can debilitate recruits if they try contemplating the entire week. "Just make it to breakfast," recruits are told, then "Just make it to lunch" and finally "Just make it to dinner."

The key is to stay in the present without thinking about the future.

This tactic is not reserved just for SEALs. Anyone can chisel away their fears by breaking seemingly insurmountable initiatives into small steps. Doing so will also provide a booster shot of confidence. "An accumulation of small successes will inspire your ability," said Thaddeus. "The giant task is a lot easier to accomplish because you have such a robust foundation of smaller tasks in your rear-view mirror."

Key Takeaway

We all experience fear when we think about the magnitude of a task or goal in its entirety. Gazing up at the top of a mountain while standing at its base is no different than considering the successful launch of a new product or initiative within a seemingly impossible time window. You can reduce your fear of failing by breaking the large task or goal into smaller, more manageable chunks and tackling each one at a time. As you complete each chunk and pass each milestone, be sure to acknowledge your success before moving onto the next part. Your confidence will slowly increase as you chug down the line to completing that previously unfeasible task.

Savage Leaders successfully achieve aggressive goals by breaking them into small, more manageable steps that will keep their fears in check.

GREET YOUR FEAR LIKE AN OLD FRIEND

Most people recoil from activities, people, and ideas they fear. Therapist and volleyball coach Dana Upton advocates doing just the opposite and works with clients to shift their relationship with fear. "To me it's accepting fear, using fear, and not overcoming fear," she told me. "Don't try to get rid of it. Rather you need to embrace it."

Dana laid down a straightforward process she uses to help her clients to accept, embrace, and turn the tables on fear. The first step is to acknowledge that fear exists. None of us are superhuman and each one of us has a unique set of fears. Fear of the unknown. Fear of negative feedback. Fear of failure. "Make peace with the fact that fear exists," Dana said. "It serves you in some way, much like sadness and anger do."

The next step, which is critical, is to change the way you look at fear by viewing it through a different lens. The point is not to pretend that fear doesn't exist, but to bring it into the light and put a name to it. Doing so creates full acceptance of and visibility into your fear. Dana says, "Greet the fear at the door and name it. Say 'Nice to meet you!'"

The next step, as Dana explains, is to get to the source of the fear. Ask yourself, "What is fear telling me?" Consider the root of the fear that is paralyzing you. For example, ask yourself, "Why do I fear this upcoming promotion?" Is it because there is a part of the role that you don't feel you're ready for? Or will the new role require you to move out of your comfort zone as an individual contributor and start managing people and their unique personalities? Look for what your fear is trying to tell you so that you can start taking action to address it.

The last step is to take action and address it head on. Use the obstacle of fear as an advantage and find a way to let it serve you. Know that it's there and use the adrenaline from it to help you focus on what you want to achieve.

Use fear to spur you into action. For example, if you are up at night sweating over your upcoming promotion to manager, become a voracious consumer of management books and podcasts to prepare for your new role. Another idea: reach out to a mentor who has made a similar transition and find out what they did to succeed, what they had to learn, what behaviors they had to adopt, what mindsets they had to shift, and what actions they took. Talk to multiple people inside and outside of your company and situation to access the roadmap to persevere and succeed in your new role.

Key Takeaway

Fear is inevitable and will emerge at different points in your life. Rather than run from it, embrace it, learn from it, and use it to your benefit. Fear is a great teacher and can also guide your actions if you can get to the root cause of it. Lean into your fears and use them to drive your growth.

Savage Leaders own the fact that fears exist, and they find ways to address them. Savage Leaders also embrace their fears to great benefit.

PREPARE FOR THE WORST AND BE READY FOR REALITY

I have a long held, deep-seated fear of sharks due to my overexposure to the *Jaws* movies. As a kid, the fear manifested itself in terror of the deep end of pools at night, and even freshwater lakes during the summer. Eventually, I (mostly) grew out of those fears, but it had prevented me from learning to surf during my childhood and early twenties while I lived in Northern California.

When I moved to Southern California in the early 2000s, I started surfing regularly though it wasn't solely due to the less "sharky" waters of L.A., Orange County, and San Diego. Living in Marina del Rey and eventually San Diego provided easy access to welcoming breaks. Living in the mecca of mainland surfing and its prevalent surf culture made the sport a regular weekend and weekday leisure activity—something I could do with friends, colleagues, and even clients.

Over the last 15 years of living and surfing in Southern California, my fear of sharks has slowly subsided, outside of spikes tied to a rare attack or sighting that was close to my home base. To me, my shark fear was nebulous—it was always there, lurking beneath the surface, both in the water and in my subconscious—but it rarely impacted me in real ways.

That all changed recently. It was 10 A.M. on a spectacular, clear summer morning, when I paddled out to surf at a break in northern San Diego with my good pal, Ricky. We've known each other since we were in high school in the Bay Area together, but we bonded after both moving to the Southland. It was midweek, so the regular mobs of weekend warriors were anchored to their desks and the surf crowd was sparse.

I had just paddled out from shore and was sitting on my board, waiting for the next set of waves. As I gazed in the distance looking for an approaching wave, I saw an enormous creature about 100 feet in front of me break the surface and launch itself out of the ocean, roll slightly backwards, and splash spectacularly into the water.

As it did, I gained a glimpse of its dark grey skin, contrasting white belly, and unmistakable arced jawline. I immediately turned to the pack of surfers to my left and asked rhetorically, "Was that a shark?"

"Uh, yeah man," they stated matter of fact. *See ya*, I thought as I did a 180° turn with my board and furiously started paddling to shore. I hadn't surfed in a few weeks, and my arms started feeling like cement sacks, but I didn't care. I kept paddling as quickly as I could toward the shore and safety. As I got about halfway, I saw Ricky paddling out.

"Shark!" I yelled as I signaled to turn around while I continued making my way to the beach. I felt calm start setting in once I waded into waist and then ankle-deep water and eventually felt my feet on the sand. "Dang, that was insane," I said to Ricky, as I caught my breath.

"Hey, do you want to surf down there?" he said as he pointed about 100 yards down the beach.

"No way, man. That was a pretty good sign I should pass today," I said as I started back to my car ready to immerse myself into the hectic workweek.

While driving home, I started reflecting on the shark incident. *Should I tell Melissa what happened?* I thought as I considered how this might erode my wife's support for me surfing whenever I needed it. I also thought about how this would impact my love for the sport. To date, surfing had become a silver bullet for fun, exercise, and relaxation. Now that this fear had moved from the realm of nebulous, perhaps even overblown at times, into a clear and present danger, I wondered if I would I be able to enjoy the one hobby that I had grown to love over the past two decades?

In processing the experience, I was surprised by how calm I felt. Despite having seen a real, live great white shark and having shared the ocean with it, I had not felt terrified or panicked. I was somewhat relieved that I didn't freeze or freak out when I experienced the worst-case scenario (well, not totally). In my fear becoming real, I faced it in real-time instead of living with the anxiety associated with my fear of seeing a great white shark—the dreaded "man in a grey suit."

In hindsight, experiencing one of my greatest fears provided me with a pathway to address other fears that may come to reality.

First, it allowed me to clearly define my fear and understand what I was afraid would happen. Now I had seen the one thing that had overwhelmed my senses in the past and could name it in my head. This experience also allowed me to formulate a plan for what to do in other similar situations and how to mitigate risks of a shark attack from occurring: don't surf after dark, avoid river mouths, and don't go in the water with active wounds.

Ultimately, having experienced one of my biggest fears prompted me to build a plan to mitigate the risks of it happening again. Knowing I had a plan helped me to relax and return to enjoying surfing. I could have given it up, but I didn't want to. Today, I continue surfing with my contingency plans and the confidence to know that should I encounter another "man in the grey suit," then I will know how to handle it.

Key Takeaway

Instead of turning a blind eye to the worst-case scenarios or our fears, we can benefit from visualizing what would happen if they did happen.

Clamming up while speaking at your national sales conference; not being able to make payroll for your team; missing your product launch date—these are terrifying possibilities. But instead of becoming paralyzed or ignoring the fear, visualizing what you would do if they occurred can actually reduce your fear and anxiety.

Once you have visualized the fear in detail, build a contingency plan for what you would do in that situation. Consider the actions you'd take, and who you could rely on to help. Also, develop a strategy and set of tactics to lower the probability of it actually coming to fruition.

Savage Leaders acknowledge their greatest fear and create plans to prevent it from coming to life and how to railroad it if it does.

THE CHALLENGE: PUT IT INTO ACTION

Don't let fear paralyze you and hold you back from taking action. When you experience fear—whether that's over an upcoming project, customer meeting, promotion, or something else—tackle it head on by doing one of the following challenges. As a bonus, you can double-down and commit to doing them all!

- **Think about what you fear and find some aspect of it that's familiar and sparks confidence and competence.** Look for some part of an upcoming project that you may have already successfully completed in the past. Consider previous customer meetings that seemed challenging at the time but yielded a successful outcome. Think about a previous promotion that prompted fear and uncertainty that you eventually tackled with ease. You likely have a win from the past that you can draw on for support now.

- **Break the big, scary project or task down into small bite-size chunks.** As you do, don't worry about its entirety. Instead focus on completing each of the steps that comprise the first part of the task. This will tamp down feelings of fear as you tighten your focus. As you successfully complete each small task, your confidence will build too. Before long, you will have completed the larger task.

- **Start by facing up to your fear and journal all of the thoughts associated with it.** Ask yourself what that fear is telling you. Are you feeling unprepared for a new role or project? Do you worry about having a challenging conversation with your boss or board of directors? Do you worry about being judged or failing? Listen to those fears, and then create a plan to tackle those fears head on. Close any skill and knowledge gaps that you see. Take practice reps in low-risk environments to get you ready. Lean into those fears and don't shy away from them. They have valuable information for you.

- **Visualize what the worst-case scenario would look like.** What would happen and who would be involved? What would be the impact on you, your team, or your company? What new opportunities could be presented? Next create a contingency plan for the worst-case scenario. Include steps you can take today to mitigate the risk of it happening.

USE YOUR PAST TO TRANSFORM THE PRESENT

"You can't connect the dots looking forward; you can only connect them looking backwards."

Steve Jobs

Our lives are a tapestry of rich stories. Stories of triumph, failure, excitement, and loss.

But often, we dismiss our stories, especially those from when we were growing up. We think of those moments as innocent forays from the past, or meaningless snapshots of our youth.

This is a missed opportunity. Our stories play an active role in defining who we are today as leaders. When we are willing to look back, we can mine our stories, using them as powerful lessons today.

Time, experience, and reflection can infuse those lessons into our own version of a Savage Leader.

Savage Leaders look deep into their pasts to extract vital lessons that apply to their lives today. For me, it was three seemingly innocent stories from growing up that as I got older, and looked back, I realized each experience had helped shape the person I am today.

In this chapter, I share those experiences.

Darren Reinke

CULTIVATE GREATER SELF-AWARENESS

In 1984, my parents decided to pull the plug on our American life and move our family to Switzerland for a year. I was flying off to happiness, or so I thought, as we took off from San Francisco on a Lufthansa 747 jet headed to Zürich, Switzerland. Despite being entrenched in my Northern California life with a crew of close friends and year-round sports and activities, I was excited by the adventure.

I didn't know it at the time, but I was embarking on a year of growth that would change the way I viewed myself and the people around me.

As a typical 9-year-old in Northern California, I was a lot like my peers. But at Schule Scherr, a German-speaking public school in the heart of Zürich, I stood out. I was the new kid. The foreign kid. The American kid.

When I arrived for my first day of school, I quickly knew that I was in for a challenge. First, in class we spoke Hochdeutsch—proper "High" German and the national language of Switzerland. On the playground, however, all the kids spoke Schweizerdeutsche, a dialect that's a different language and one that Germans can't understand.

I had to learn two languages, fast and in real time, if I was going to have any chance of fitting in and making friends.

I also had to deal with bullies. One morning, when I walked onto the school grounds, I was struck on my cheek, about an inch from my eye, by what felt like a hot coal. I felt blood stream down my face.

Who shot that thing at me? I thought, feeling panicked and afraid, while filled with adrenaline.

In a bold and defensive reaction, I gave "the bird" to the older boys, who I thought had hit me with a rock from a slingshot. But no one owned up to shooting me. As I stared into the sea of kids across the playground, I felt like it was me against the world. Being an outsider in a foreign land, felt very cold, isolating.

After that low point, my life at Schule Scherr slowly improved as I learned German at a rapid clip through total immersion in third grade and daily private tutoring sessions with my teacher, Fraulein Buhler and my ex-pat compatriot, Rui from South Africa.

Eventually, I earned respect in class with my strong, overcompensating math skills. I still received a sea of red marks on any writing assignment. Excelling in basketball, a sport that wasn't nearly as popular among Swiss kids, also helped build my "playground cred," though the occasional scrap would break out as I continued to earn respect from the other kids.

My sister, Kara dragged me along with her and her Swiss friends while I started to make friends and get acclimated. (I'll be forever grateful for that, Kara!)

By the end of the year, I had made several friends, developed a "crush" or two, and eventually earned the respect of my peers. More importantly, the year in a Swiss public school helped me experience living as an outsider—culturally and linguistically. While I was able to fit in quickly, the experience forged a sense of appreciation and empathy for people from different cultures and backgrounds as well as the importance of inclusion.

Living in Switzerland also created greater self-awareness. Awareness of the multitude of different perspectives and opinions of people around the globe. I learned that not everyone shares the same views as Americans. It also taught me greater awareness of my own actions and their impact on others.

I didn't realize all of this at nine-years old, but looking back as an adult, I see how that was a formative year for me and instilled important lessons that developed who I am, and who I want to be at my core.

Key Takeaway

Savage Leaders understand that we don't all see the world through the same lens.

Through a trying year, I learned the importance of self-awareness and that my personal values, beliefs, and experiences might not always be the same as those of the people around me. Greater self-awareness makes it easier to walk in other peoples' shoes, to see and even experience their perspective. This can lead to greater empathy, understanding, and ultimately, the ability to form better relationships.

Don't assume your team and colleagues think, feel, or experience the world the same way as you. Try putting yourself in their shoes to better understand how they might feel in a situation or in response to change.

Also, make personal reflection and introspection a regular part of your week to ensure you become more aware of the changes occurring inside of you. Consider your recent interactions with others to identify ways to improve how you show up, communicate, and engage with your team members.

Savage Leaders cultivate greater awareness of self and others and appreciate the differences that make up a team, company, and community.

LEAD BY EXAMPLE

Growing up, I gravitated toward leadership roles in sports. Leadership in youth sports was primarily focused on motivating my fellow teenagers, whose attention tended to drift to what was happening that weekend, or to the girls in the stands, and parents and friends cheering on the sidelines. It was my job to lead by example and show the level of effort needed not only to compete, but to *win*.

One of my earliest memories of leading by example, or shall I say, *not* leading by example, occurred during the first half of a basketball game against our archrival, Tamalpais. Prior to this game, our season had been off to a brilliant start. We enjoyed a six-game winning streak, multiple pre-season tournament victories, and personally, I had never played better. In one tournament, featuring future NBA players including Michael "Yogi" Stewart, I even earned an all-tournament nomination.

Against Tamalpais, though we were playing our worst game of the year. As a team, we struggled to find any cohesiveness on offense, and we lacked a sense of urgency to do the hard work, play defense and rebound. While heading back to the bench after our team called a timeout, my frustration got the best of me. I kicked the rack of water bottles so hard that they sprayed several teammates and spectators seated in the front two rows.

As soon as it happened, I realized that I had made a huge mistake. I hadn't modeled the role of a team captain and leader. My teammates saw one of their leaders falling apart and our collective frustration continued to build. We failed to recover. We lost the game and it set the stage for what became an unsuccessful season, after having started off with so much promise.

Worse, I had fallen short of being a leader.

Key Takeaway

It's easy (and lazy) for leaders to think, "do as I say, don't do as I do." But that is not leadership. Savage Leaders keenly focus on modeling the behaviors they want to see among their team members.

Although my basketball experience happened to me when I was young, it stuck with me, because I had failed myself, and I knew it. I knew I was better than kicking water bottles in frustration, and I never wanted to let down myself—or my teams—in the future.

I've carried this lesson with me since. I learned from my mistake, and now I work hard to lead by example in work and in life, by demonstrating the behaviors I want to see from my teams, my kids, and even my clients. Channeling my inner Gandhi, I realized the importance of, "being the leader that you want to see in the world."

Colleagues observe and often mirror our behaviors, both positive and negative. Be sure that you exhibit the behaviors you want to see in your team and organization. Use self-reflection to assess your behaviors and recognize any changes you need to make in order to embody the shifts you want to see within yourself and your team. Commit to making those changes. Action is what matters, not words or proclamations.

Savage Leaders lead by example and model the hard-to-achieve behaviors required for enduring success.

PUT IN THE HARD WORK

As I started high school, my life began revolving around school, girls, and sports—though not necessarily in that order. Getting my schoolwork done was a given. My parents and grandparents had long engrained in me the need for education to open doors and opportunities in life. Chasing girls, on the other hand, was fruitless given my 13-year-old scrawny frame and short stature compared to the upper classman, who made our female classmates swoon and invited them to prom.

Naturally, sports became a big focus right out of the gate for me. Year-round baseball and basketball provided me with an outlet for fun while helping me to forge lifelong friendships, gain confidence, and to teach me how to work with different teammates. Sports also taught me the criticality of hard work.

Baseball was my first love. I developed a passion for the game from my Little League coach, Roger Firenze, and I had a knack for hitting. As I proceeded through my high school years, I coasted on my natural ability and made the JV team, won MVP as a sophomore on the JV squad, and eventually earned a spot on the Varsity team in my junior year. It wasn't exactly big-league baseball, but I felt a sense of accomplishment.

After biding my time during my junior year on the Varsity team, I was ready to breakthrough as a senior and earn a starting spot. I showed up for fall baseball—a relaxed league intended to keep our skills sharp between seasons—but I lacked the passion for the game that I had possessed as a younger kid.

Was I burned out or was it the coaches who failed to inspire me to work hard?

Regardless, the spark was missing after having loved the sport for many years. I checked the box and showed up to practice and for the games, but I didn't spend extra time practicing fielding grounders and fly balls or taking extra swings in the batting cage.

When spring rolled around, I looked forward to the season, confident I would finish my high school career on a high note. My passion returned as I showed up to practice and played alongside my close friends, Clyde, Billy, and Jimmy. As the season wore on, though I was in and out of the starting lineup. I struggled to find any rhythm at the plate or in the field. At the end of the season, we entered the playoffs with a chance to win the league title.

Unfortunately for me, I was firmly planted on the bench with few opportunities to get on the field.

Prior to the championship game, my coach read off the starting lineup. I was in it! Excitement rippled through me, until I heard there was a catch. I would play right field, but a designated hitter (a player who only hits in the game for one designated field player) would hit for me. I felt crushed and also confused. Hitting had always been my forte while fielding fly balls was a constant adventure.

I played the entire game in a losing effort and walked off the field with my head hanging low. I trudged across the parking lot feeling dejected and humiliated, as I walked past the same parents who had seen me excel in baseball my entire life. It was the low point of my sports career.

At the time, I blamed the coaches for failing to give me the benefit of the doubt and not giving me any breaks. Whether or not that was true, I'll never know, but as the years went by and I looked back, I've come to realize that I have to take ownership of my failures.

I had failed. My lack of playing time was (partly) my fault. I had failed to put in the hard work to beat out the competition. I had failed to put in the time and do the extra practice reps—fielding balls in the outfield and spending time in the batting cage.

I have vowed to never let a lack of hard work get in the way of achieving my goals. It is about doing everything I can, giving my best to succeed.

Key Takeaway

Talent alone isn't enough. Savage Leaders know that. Hard work is critical to transform our natural abilities into real strengths. Prepping for job interviews, studying before a client meeting, taking action and not leaving anything up to chance or someone else's subjective point of view—these efforts separate Savage Leaders from others. Passion is great, but effort is critical to turn our passions and abilities into real successes.

No matter what you aim to achieve, put in the hard work. Don't coast on your talent or resume alone. Always work, always grind. Don't diminish the competition when you are out in front. Put in the effort to beat out the competition. Hard work, expertise, and talent win out.

Savage Leaders commit to hard work to transform natural ability into towering strengths that enable long-term success.

THE CHALLENGE: PUT IT INTO PRACTICE

We all have stories. Some insignificant, but many transformative. When we look to our pasts, they can help us become better leaders today.

What are your stories? Are there some that you dismissed as innocent forays of youth? What are they? How have they formed your core, and how do they drive you to become great today?

Take a few minutes to write down two or three memorable stories from your past. Capture the key details. What was it about each story that made them memorable? Did you overcome an obstacle or achieve something you didn't think you were capable of? Did you fail for the first time?

Most importantly, write down what you learned from each experience.

Finally, identify opportunities to integrate each learning into your personal journey to become a Savage Leader. How can you take the lesson and apply it to your life today?

CONCLUSION

THE FUTURE OF THE SAVAGE LEADER

"Life moves pretty fast. If you don't stop and look around once in a while, you could miss it."

Ferris Bueller in 1980s film, *Ferris Bueller's Day Off*

Our lives and careers move quickly.

It's important that we enjoy each and every day, but we also don't want to let time pass as we wait for the perfect moment to start growing and getting better. My hope is that you have already started to put some of the Savage Principles into practice and have seen results.

Different principles will be relevant at different points in your life, so be sure to return to the stories and challenges when you need them. For example, fear and doubt might be your biggest impediment in your career today, but there may come a point when you need to revisit your values and beliefs.

Use the Savage Leader as both a source of inspiration as well as a quick guide to grow and improve.

Writing and publishing this book forced me to rely on many of the Savage Principles. It has also been the next step in a journey that I started over four decades ago. My personal commitment is for this not to be my only book, rather my *first* book. But this is only part of my journey. I'm constantly looking for tips and techniques, and mindsets to help me improve how I show up as a leader and person.

Like each one of us, the Savage Principles will grow and evolve over time, and I'll continue defining, testing, refining, and applying them on my path to achieving my personal definition of greatness. I commit to using them each day to be a better dad, a better husband, a better leader, and a better person.

What about you? What do you commit to? What do you aspire to do, be, and experience?

I want to hear from you. Send me your feedback on how the Savage Principles work in your life. Share with me how you're applying them and what changes you're witnessing. Tell me about how the Savage Principles have helped you on your journey to being great, whatever that may be.

We're on this road together, so please share your triumphs as well as your struggles with me. I'm here to support you on your path. Email me at darren.reinke@groupsixty.com or connect via @groupsixty on social media.

I truly believe that inside of you lies a Savage Leader, capable of achieving extraordinary goals and reaching your definition of greatness.

You can do this.

I'm rooting for you.

READER BONUS: THE SAVAGE LEADER FIELD GUIDE

The Savage Leader includes dozens of practices designed to help you bring the Savage Principles to life. To help you on this journey, I've created a *free* bonus: *The Savage Leader Field Guide*. To access your guide, visit thesavageleader.com today.

SOURCES

SAVAGE PRINCIPLE #1: USE VALUES TO ANCHOR AND GUIDE YOU

Dana Upton, phone interview with author, March 21, 2018.

Kurt Kaufer, in-person interview with author, March 9, 2018.

Evan Mendelsohn, in-person interview with author, August 24, 2017.

Web.com. "Secrets of Success: Evan Mendelsohn." Accessed June 3, 2020. https://www.web.com/blog/the-spotlight/success-stories/secrets-of-success-evan-mendelsohn

Tipssyelves.com. Accessed June3, 2020. https://www.tipsyelves .com/blog/tipsy-elves-founders-evan-and-nick/

SAVAGE PRINCIPLE #2: ADAPT BEST PRACTICES FOR AUTHENTICITY

Kevin J. Ryan. "Elon Musk's 6 Habits for Staying Insanely Productive." *Inc.*, February 10, 2017. https://www.inc.com/kevin-j-ryan/ss/elon-musk-habits-to-staying-productive.html

"Multitasking: Switching costs." American Psychological Association, March 20, 2006. http://www.apa.org/research/action/multitask.aspx

SAVAGE PRINCIPLE #3: FORGE UNBREAKABLE BONDS WITH YOUR TRIBE

Grazer, Brian, and Charles Fishman, *A Curious Mind: The Secret to a Bigger Life*, New York: Simon & Schuster, (2015).

Navid Alipour, interview with the author, June 25, 2018.

Husman, R. C., Lahiff, J. M., & Penrose, J. M., *Business Communication: Strategies and Skills,* Chicago: Dryden Press, 1988.

Berger, Warren, *A More Beautiful Question: The Power of Inquiry to Spark Breakthrough Ideas*. Bloomsbury USA, 2014.

Natraj, "Question is More Important than the Answer," RE-LEARNING, April 24, 2014, https://www.myklassroom.com/blog/question-is-more-important-than-the-answer/

SAVAGE PRINCIPLE #4: COMMIT TO LIFELONG LEARNING AND GROWTH

Tom Spengler, interview with the author, August 15, 2017.

Trevor Murphy, interview with the author, April 24, 2018.

Phil Dana, interview with the author, February 16, 2018.

NBA Player, interview with the author, September 16, 2018.

Hubie Brown, "How Would I Coach Against Him? Hubie Brown on Jordan." NBA.com, Accessed May 1, 2020. http://archive.nba.com/jordan/hubieonjordan.html

Wikipedia, "List of National Basketball Association Annual Scoring Leaders." Accessed May 1, 2020, https://en.wikipedia.org/wiki/List_of_National_Basketball_Association_annual_scoring_leaders

SAVAGE PRINCIPLE #5: PRACTICE MENTAL AND PHYSICAL REPS TO WIN WHEN IT COUNTS

Avery Yang, "Why Jaylen Brown Is Among NBA Players Using Mental Skills App Lucid," *SportTechie*, September 6, 2017, https://www.sporttechie.com/celtics-jaylen-brown-nba-players-mental-skills-app-lucid/

TED. "Your body language may shape who you are." Accessed May 4, 2020. https://www.ted.com/talks/amy_cuddy_your_body_language_may_shape_who_you_are?language=en

Dana Upton, interview with the author, March 21, 2018.

NBA Player, interview with the author, September 16, 2018.

SAVAGE PRINCIPLE #6: TAKE ACTION TO MAINTAIN AND REGAIN FOCUS

Jamie Green, interview with the author, June 21, 2018.

Melanie Curtin, "Science: This 1Daily Habit Lowers Stress, Boosts Your Immune System, and Improves Focus." *Inc.*, January 10, 2017, https://www.inc.com/melanie-curtin/want-to-improve-your-focus-and-lower-stress-in-2017-science-says-to-take-up-this.html

SAVAGE PRINCIPLE #7: DIG DEEP TO PERSEVERE IN DARK TIMES

Trevor Glavin, interview with the author, April 24, 2018.

Anonymous, interview with the author, June 15, 2018.

Rebecca Aydin, "How 3 guys turned renting air mattresses in their apartment into a $31 billion company, Airbnb." *Business Insider*, September 20, 2019, https://www.businessinsider.com/how-airbnb-was-founded-a-visual-history-2016-2#the-year-was-2007-and-roommates-joe-gebbia-and-brian-chesky-couldnt-afford-their-san-francisco-rent-1

SAVAGE PRINCIPLE #8: EMBRACE AND UTILIZE PATIENCE AS A SECRET WEAPON

Brian Smith, interview with the author, April 16, 2018.

Brian Smith, *The Birth of a Brand*, Beyond Words Publishing, (2013).

Billy McKnight, interview with the author, March 29, 2018.

SAVAGE PRINCIPLE #9: SEEK OUT DISCOMFORT TO DRIVE GROWTH

Thaddeus Siwinski, interview with the author, August 30, 2018.

Amir Sarhangi, interview with the author, September 6, 2019.

SAVAGE PRINCIPLE #10: OWN AND CHALLENGE LIMITING BELIEFS

Michel Kripalani, interview with the author, April 24, 2018.

SAVAGE PRINCIPLE #11: CRUSH YOUR DOUBTS AND REFRAME THEM FOR SUCCESS

Big Think, "Michael Strahan: How to Overcome Self Doubt," YouTube Video, 3:03, November 16, 2015, https://www .youtube.com/watch?v=vqfyEh8HDYM

Biography, "Michael Strahan: How to Overcome Self Doubt." Accessed April 27, 2018, https://www.biography.com/athlete/ michael-strahan

Pro Football Reference, "Michael Strahan Overview," Accessed April 27, 2018. https://www.pro-football-reference.com/ players/S/StraMi02.htm

SAVAGE PRINCIPLE #12: MAKE FEAR YOUR FRIEND

Thaddeus Siwinski, interview with the author, August 30, 2018.

Dana Upton, interview with the author, March 21, 2018.

SAVAGE PRINCIPLE #13: USE YOUR PAST TO TRANSFORM THE PRESENT

N/A

ACKNOWLEDGEMENTS

Writing a book was one of the biggest challenges of my life. Committing to publishing it was a completely separate endeavor as it forced me to be vulnerable in the court of internet opinion, to be evaluated, judged, and criticized. I wouldn't have been able to succeed in completing this project without the many special people in my life—family, friends, mentors, clients, and many other amazing people whom I've met along the way.

Thank you, Dana Upton for the original spark to write this book. "Darren, it sounds like you are going to write a book?!" was a statement (or perhaps a question) that kicked off this entire journey and sparked the sense of possibility.

To David Shapiro—for being my "provocateur" at the outset and for "pushing the rock back down the hill" when all I wanted to do was finish this project. Your support and insight, while pushing me to be bold and provocative, has been instrumental in making my writing more insightful and engaging.

Thank you to Amanda Ibey for believing in me and this project, for helping me to push this book over the finish line, and for teaching me to be a better writer.

Thank you to all the Savage Leaders who generously spent time sharing your stories with me: Kurt Kaufer, Evan Mendelsohn, Navid Alipour, Tom Spengler, Trevor Murphy, Phil Dana, Dana Upton, Jamie Green, Trevor Glavin, Brian Smith, Billy McKnight, Thaddeus Siwinski, Amir Sarhangi, and Michel Kripalani.

Thank you to my parents for providing me with a bedrock of values upon which I have lived my life, and for your unwavering support through all the endeavors that I have embarked on when surely there was a safer, more secure path.

To my sister, Kara for being there during the tough times of childhood and beyond when things weren't always going my way. And for toughening me up until the "tent brawl" tipped the tide.

To Melissa, my beautiful and supportive wife, for being there through all the ups and downs. You are the rock that anchors me.

Finally, to our boys, Madden and Kai. You inspire me to do better and be better. I would never ask you to do anything that I wouldn't. Thanks for pushing me to be my best.

AUTHOR BIO

Darren Reinke fundamentally believes there is greatness within each one of us. His mission is to unleash the inner lion within leaders so that they can lead a more authentic and joyful life while creating stronger and more resilient teams, organizations, and communities.

Darren founded Group Sixty, an executive coaching and training company based in San Diego, to bring his purpose to life and to transform leaders, their teams, and their organizations.

Darren works with leaders and teams at Fortune 500's, mid-market companies, fast-growing startups, visionary non-profits, and transitioning military veterans. The common thread is three-fold: his clients have a desire to be great; they are willing to be introspective; and they are committed to putting in the work to change and grow.

Darren shares his thoughts on leadership and life on Instagram (@groupsixty), Twitter (@groupsixty), and LinkedIn (@Darren Reinke).